What a Character!

AMERICA'S FAMOUS SPIES

Notable Lives from History

Marilyn Boyer

First printing: April 2024
Third printing: July 2025

Master Books, P.O. Box 726, Green Forest, AR 72638

Master Books® is a division of the New Leaf Publishing Group, LLC.

ISBN: 978-1-68344-363-6
ISBN: 978-1-61458-878-8 (digital)
Library of Congress Control Number: 2024932930

Cover: Diana Bogardus
Interior: Terry White

Please consider requesting that a copy of this volume be purchased by your local library system.

Printed in the United States of America

Please visit our website for other great titles:
www.masterbooks.com

For information regarding promotional opportunities,
please contact the publicity department at pr@nlpg.com.

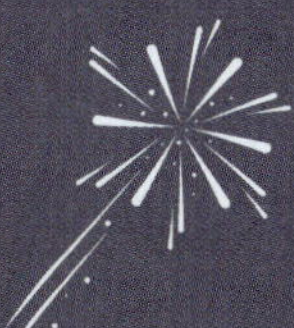

Table of Contents

Image Credits

Images are AI-generated at shutterstock.com

Maps:

Map Trek: Atlas of the World & U.S. History – pages 6, 64, and 102

American War of Independence

In the late 18th century, the thirteen American colonies were fed up with British rule and taxation without representation. The flames of revolution were ignited, leading to a daring struggle for independence.

Visionaries like Thomas Jefferson and brave leaders like George Washington emerged, guiding a diverse group of colonists in their quest for freedom. The American War of Independence marked a defining moment in history, culminating in the birth of a new nation, the United States of America. During the war there were secret missions, cunning disguises, and hidden messages that played a crucial role in the fight for independence. This was the era of spies, brave individuals who risked everything to gather information and outsmart the enemy.

After seven years of fighting for freedom, the colonies successfully gained their independence and created a brand new country. In 1789, they officially approved the Constitution, marking the beginning of the United States of America.

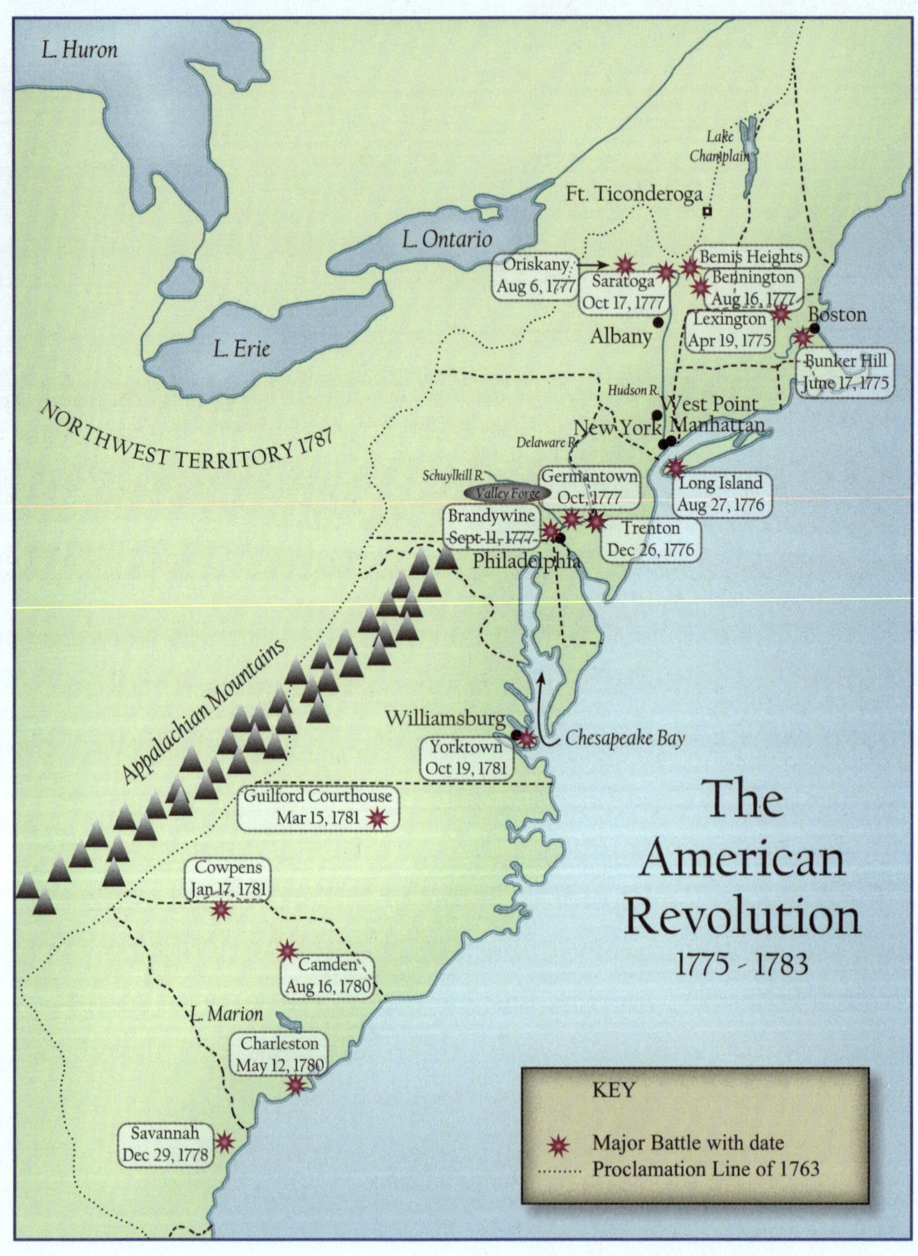

1

Nathan Hale—Spy and Hero

September, 1776	American War of Independence

During the American Revolution, both the British and Patriot armies needed spies to gather information about the enemy. Spies would find out the number of soldiers the enemy had and where they were located, as well as how much ammunition and how many supplies the enemy had available. Each side especially needed to learn of the enemy's plans to march or attack. Spies had to try to learn as much information as possible without the enemy knowing what they were doing. Spies also had to be really smart. They'd use secret codes to send messages back to their own side. Spying was dangerous, and both sides knew it. But these brave individuals believed in the cause so much that they risked everything to help their side win.

Off to College

If you had lived in the colony of Connecticut in 1769, you might have seen two young men riding away from their farm home on horseback. They were Nathan and Enoch Hale, and they were on their way to Yale College. Nathan was only 14 years old. In those days, that was a common age for boys who went to leave home if they went to college. His father and mother worked hard on their farm to feed their 12 children. The children worked hard, too. Everyone had to help on the farm. The children were taught from the Bible and the family prayed together daily. The

parents finally managed to save enough money to send Enoch and Nathan to Yale University. Nathan liked college, and he was a good student. He loved to read. He liked the stories of heroes from the past. He dreamed of doing great deeds himself someday.

Nathan also loved the outdoors. He was a good runner and jumper, and he did well in the contests he had with the other young men. He was a good wrestler, too. He was a kind young man; most people liked him. Nathan and his college friends were growing and changing. America was changing, too. In those days America was not a nation. It was just 13 British **colonies** spread up and down the eastern part of North America. They could not make their own laws because they were ruled by King George of England. They lived in colonial America, but they were still Englishmen.

Trouble with England

King George made laws for the colonists without listening to them about their needs. He made them pay high taxes. He did many things that were not fair to his people in America. Many people in the colonies were angry. As time went on, they got even more upset. The colonists asked the king for relief from laws he made that cost the colonists a lot of money

colonies: Areas under the full or partial political control of another country

and commanded control over their businesses and lives. But the king wanted more money to pay for his wars and didn't respect the colonists even though they were his subjects.

In 1773, Nathan finished college and became a schoolteacher. His students liked him because he was a good teacher. They knew he wanted to help them learn. He expected the children to be respectful and follow the school rules, but he wanted them to have fun, too. Sometimes he would do tricks for them, showing them how well he could run and jump. Nathan was happy teaching. He might have remained a schoolteacher for the rest of his life if something hadn't happened that changed Connecticut forever. In fact, it changed the world. A war started.

On April 19, 1775, there was a fight between British soldiers and the colonists at Lexington and Concord in Massachusetts. The Massachusetts men believed that America should be free from England and its king. They had been storing up weapons and gunpowder at Concord. The British soldiers had marched out of Boston and through Lexington on their way to capture the supplies at Concord. When they reached Lexington, the men of the town came out to protect their homes. They did not plan to shoot at the soldiers unless the British tried to harm them or their homes. Someone — no one is sure if he was British or a Patriot — fired a shot. Then all the soldiers began shooting at the colonists. Several of the Lexington men were hurt or killed.

There was another battle at Concord. Riders were carrying the news around the countryside and the farmers were gathering from all around to fight against the British. Soon there were so many Patriots shooting that the soldiers turned around and ran. The farmers chased them all the way to Boston. When the news reached Connecticut, the people gathered in town meetings to talk about war. Nathan went to one of these meetings with his neighbors. Some of the people were afraid to fight. They knew the British had many soldiers. They also had plenty of money to buy weapons and supplies. The Patriots had no army and little money.

Some people at the meeting thought they should just make peace with England. Others said that the British government was wrong to rule the colonies unfairly. They must fight for their rights as Englishmen. And if the King would not treat them fairly, they should separate from England and start a new nation. Nathan was one of those who wanted to fight for freedom. When it was his turn to speak, he stood up and shouted, "Let us march at once and never lay down our arms until we obtain our independence!"[1] He wanted to become a soldier right away, but he had to finish the school year with his students.

One day Nathan received a letter. He was being asked to be an officer in the new Patriot army! Nathan was excited. He would be a leader of other soldiers. On the last day of school, Nathan shook the hand of each student and said his last goodbyes. He was sad to leave his young friends. They were sad also as they watched him leave. They hoped he would be safe as he fought for his country.

Becoming A Ranger

Soon, Nathan joined General Washington and the Patriot army in Boston. Nathan and the other officers drilled their men over and over. They worked hard to learn to fight well together. Washington had the British **bottled up** in the town, and he hoped they would give up and sail away. Nathan wished they would come out and have a battle. He wanted to do more to help his country.

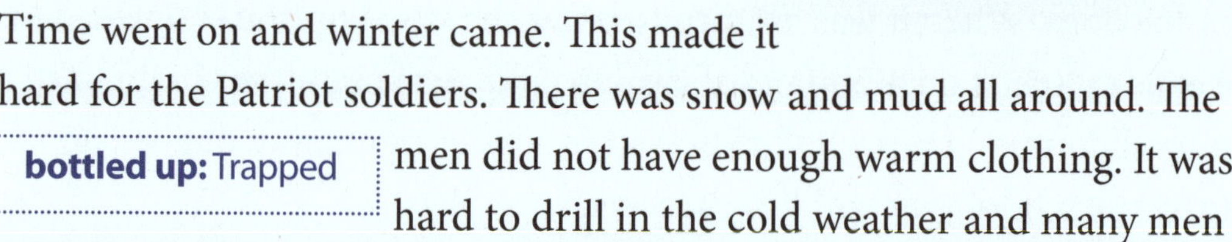

Time went on and winter came. This made it hard for the Patriot soldiers. There was snow and mud all around. The men did not have enough warm clothing. It was hard to drill in the cold weather and many men got sick. Nathan visited his sick men in their tents and prayed with them. He tried to cheer them up, but many men were giving up and going home to care for their farms and families. In order to keep his men with him, Nathan shared his pay with them.

bottled up: Trapped

Nathan was made a captain in January 1776. He was responsible for leading many men into battle. After the Battle of Dorchester Heights in March, the British gave up Boston and marched down to their ships in the harbor. As they sailed away, General Washington thought they would go to the colony of New York to make their next attack. Nathan and many other soldiers were sent there to defend it. As Nathan looked out across New York from his camp, he could see British ships in the East River. Some of them were big battleships.

One was a small ship called a **sloop**. It was loaded with guns and other supplies. The Patriot army needed those things badly. As Nathan looked at the sloop sitting peacefully in the water, he had an idea. He thought he saw a way he could do something important to help the American cause.

When night came, Nathan and some of his men got into a rowboat. Being careful not to splash with their oars, the men paddled quietly to the sloop. It was near a massive warship called the *Asia*. If the sailors on the big ship heard them, they would shoot the Americans and sink their boat, but the Patriots were very careful. They got to the sloop and quietly climbed aboard. They took the British sailors on the sloop prisoner. The elated Americans sailed the sloop across the river to their army. The Patriots were overjoyed to get a ship full of things they badly needed! Soon Nathan was asked to join the Rangers, an **elite** group of soldiers who carried out specialized tasks for General Washington. Nathan hoped he would soon have another chance to do something great for freedom.

sloop: Small sailing warship

elite: Superior in training and abilities

A Special, Dangerous Mission

In September 1776, the four Captains of the Rangers received a request. Colonel Thomas Knowlton called them to a meeting. He needed a volunteer to do a job that would be extremely hard and dangerous. Things were looking bad for the Patriots after the British

had beaten them at a battle in Long Island the month before. General Washington needed to know how many British soldiers were in New York, and where they were. When would they attack the Americans again? Colonel Knowlton looked grim. He needed a **spy**.

But no one wanted to be a spy. People thought spying wasn't honorable. Brave men were willing to fight and die in battle, but spying meant sneaking around and hiding, trying to fool the enemy instead of defeating him in a fair fight. A spy did not wear his uniform, but regular clothes. If he were caught, he would likely be hung. The young officers looked unhappy. They wanted to fight for freedom, but spying? That wasn't honorable. They looked around the room, not wanting to look Colonel Knowlton in the eye. Nathan could not offer to take the mission because he was recovering from a serious illness and was still quite weak. So, the colonel did not get his volunteer that night.

spy: Person who secretly reports information on activities, movements, and plans of an enemy

It wasn't long before Colonel Knowlton called his captains again. General Washington still needed a spy. Who was brave enough to risk his life? Nathan was no longer weak. He stepped forward and stood before Colonel Knowlton. "I will go, sir," he said firmly. The general had his spy!

Nathan told his friend, William Hull, what he planned to do. He would **disguise** himself as a schoolteacher and sneak into the British camp. He

disguise: Alter one's dress or appearance to conceal one's true identity

would pretend to be a teacher traveling around, looking for a school to teach. That would give him a reason for going from place to place while he wrote notes about the British army and their camps.

William did not like the idea at all. A spy? Why, spying was like lying or cheating. He thought Nathan would lose the respect of his friends if he did this. And Nathan was too honest for a spy. He would be found out and killed by the British. "Don't do this, Nathan!" William begged.

Nathan explained to William that he had to go. General Washington needed to know what the enemy was up to. "I wish to be useful," he explained.[2] Yes, spying was dangerous, but it was not dishonorable. He confided in William that he longed to be useful and that every kind of service for the public good was honorable by being necessary. As the two friends shook hands, Nathan promised William that he would think it over. It is never easy for a young man to do something his friends think is wrong. Nathan knew William was only trying to help him with his advice. He also knew that many other people agreed with William. However, General Washington and his country needed him. He would do this job no matter what.

Danger on Long Island

Soon Nathan was on his way across the water to Long Island. He left his uniform and sword in the camp and wore a plain coat and hat, like a wandering schoolteacher. In his disguise, he roamed around the island. How many soldiers did the British have? Where were they placed? How many cannons did they have? General Washington needed to know. Carefully, Nathan wrote notes and drew maps. He hid his papers in his shoes. For about nine days, Nathan walked about the camps. Then he started back toward the Patriot camp. Somehow, he was captured. Some thought it may have been his **Tory** cousin who saw and reported him. The British searched him and found his notes and maps in his shoes. Nathan knew he was in deep trouble.

He was brought to General William Howe, the highest-ranking officer in the British army in New York. He asked Nathan who he was and why he was in the British camps. Nathan was an honest man. He could have tried to save himself by lying, but Nathan told the truth. He admitted he was an American soldier and a spy for General Washington. The British officer's face grew red with anger. A spy in his camp! He ordered Nathan to be hanged the very next morning.

Tory: American colonist who supported the British side during the American Revolution

Nathan was locked in a building near the General's office. There was no chance to escape because a soldier guarded the door. He tried to prepare himself to die the next day. He thought about his family back home. He thought about his country and about God. He hoped that America would win her freedom someday.

Nathan asked for a Bible. He asked for a minister to visit him in his last hours. The British officer in charge said no to both requests. How cruel! Nathan was given paper and ink to write letters. He wrote to his family and to Colonel Knowlton. Instead of sending the letters, the British officer destroyed them. He was determined to let Nathan have nothing but a hangman's rope.

When morning came, Nathan Hale was taken outside. He knew that he would die this morning, but he was not afraid to die. When the British officer asked if he had any last words, Nathan replied, "I only regret that I have but one life to lose for my country."[3] Though the young soldier's life was ended, the story of his heroic courage had just begun. For many, many years boys and girls all over America memorized and quoted his last words. A statue of him was placed at Yale College where he had studied as a boy.

Nathan Hale did not succeed in his mission to get news of the British for General Washington. He did not live to go on and win battles. However, though he is not commemorated for a great victory, he is for being a great man of character. He was willing to face great danger for his country. He was willing even to give up his life. He did not live to see his dream of freedom come true, but a grateful nation looks back even today with deep respect for Nathan Hale, a true American hero.

2

Lydia Darragh – Quaker Spy

December 1777	Philadelphia, Pennsylvania

In September 1777, General William Howe, leading the British army, marched into Philadelphia, the seat of the Continental Congress. The Continental Congress was the ruling body set up in 1774 by American colonial leaders to determine how to proceed with opposition to unfair British rule. He took up residence there until the following spring. Many Patriot residents, businessmen of the city, and the Continental Congress abandoned the city before their arrival. Howe hoped that by seizing Philadelphia, he would rally the Loyalists in the colony of Pennsylvania, discourage the rebels by capturing their capital, and bring the war to a speedy conclusion. This also allowed British troops a comfortable place to spend the winter, forcing residents to allow them to occupy local homes.

Washington's troops spent six weeks at Whitemarsh Township, which was 13 miles northwest of Philadelphia. The army began building **redoubts** to be ready if Howe attacked. From here Washington could **monitor** the British movements in Philadelphia as well as protect his supply cities in the west.

redoubts: Temporary fortifications

monitor: Keep an eye on

Howe's Headquarters

General Howe set up his headquarters in Philadelphia at the home of Colonel John Cadwalader (a prominent Patriot) across the street from the large house of a quiet Quaker family, the Darraghs. Quakers were gentle people who dressed plainly and

opposed any form of violence. They were not expected to fight on either side in the war. William Darragh, age 56, was the son of a clergyman. He was a teacher who was skilled in **shorthand**. He and his wife Lydia, age 48, had five children at the time. She occasionally served as a nurse and **midwife**. Since the Darraghs' house was so spacious and well-suited for the purpose, General Howe often made use of one of the rooms there to hold important meetings with his officers. Howe knew the Darraghs were Quakers, but he didn't know their oldest son Charles, age 22, had joined Washington's army and was stationed at Whitemarsh. He also didn't suspect that Lydia was a Patriot at heart.

shorthand: Method of rapid writing by using abbreviations and symbols

midwife: Delivers babies

Howe's Important Meeting

On December 2, 1777, a British officer and spy, Major John Andre, entered her parlor and asked Lydia to have the room they used as a conference room ready for an important meeting at 8:00 that evening. He also instructed her to have all the family in bed by then. He told her he would let her know when the meeting was over so she could **extinguish** the fire and lock the doors. Lydia prepared the conference room, welcomed the officers, and as requested, got her family off to bed. Lydia, however, was not able to sleep. Thinking of her son Charles and the

extinguish: Put out

Patriot army shivering with cold at the nearby Whitemarsh camp, she slipped quietly out of bed and crept noiselessly down the hall. Entering a linen closet located next to the conference room she heard General Howe reading his order. He had learned from his spies that the Patriots were planning to move camp. The British plan was to ambush them at Whitemarsh late on the evening of December 4. Surely, considering their larger force and catching the Patriot army unprepared, it would be a certain victory for the British. Lydia, shivering with fright, dashed back down the hall and lay down in her bed, wondering how she could get this information to Washington in time to help not only her son Charles but the entire cause for freedom.

Lydia's Dilemma

Soon thereafter, Lydia heard a loud knock on her bedroom door. Knowing it was Major Andre, she lay there, not answering until the third knock, pretending to be in a deep sleep. When she opened the door, acting very sleepy, Andre commented that she must be a sound sleeper as he had knocked three times trying to wake her. He told her the meeting had ended, so she could put out the fire and lock her door. Lydia said goodnight to the officers, locked the door, put out the fire and candles, then made her way back to bed. Lydia's mind raced trying to decide what she should do.

When morning came, Lydia matter-of-factly told her husband that their flour supply was getting low and that she would go to the mill today to buy more. Lydia crossed the street to Howe's headquarters and requested a pass to leave the city to go to the mill at Frankford. Going to the flour mill was not an unusual thing for a housewife to do so she had no trouble in obtaining a pass to go through British lines. She carried her empty sack and walked the eight miles on foot through light snow. Reaching the gristmill, she left the sack with the miller to be filled and told him she would pick it up later that day.

The American Camp

Lydia set off on foot, heading in the direction of the American camp at Whitemarsh. Soon, she heard a horse approaching and looked up to see Lieutenant Colonel John Craig, one of Washington's **light brigade**, a man she had met once before. Greatly surprised to see her he asked, "Why Mrs. Darragh, what are you doing so far from home?"[4] Lydia requested that he walk beside her, which he did, leading his

light brigade: Officers that travel light and fast

horse by his side. In **hushed** tones, she told him the important intelligence she was risking her life to deliver. He, without hesitation, led her to the eating establishment where Elias Boudinot, **Commissary of Prisoners**, was eating his breakfast. Questioning him about flour, she thrust in his hand a dirty **needle book**. Surprised, he began to flip through its many pockets until he came to the last one where he found a slip of rolled-up paper. As he read the note, he learned the vital information that Howe was coming with 5,000 men, 13 cannons, baggage wagons, and 11 boats on wheels.

hushed: Quiet

Commissary of Prisoners: Office established to handle prisoners and find intelligence

needle book: Fabric book for keeping sewing needles

Boudinot and Craig suggested that Lydia go to a nearby house where she would be given some food before her trip home, then galloped off to Washington's headquarters. Lydia requested that they deliver the information, but not reveal the source, to protect her identity. She was determined to get home before dark, so Lydia did not stop for food or rest but trudged on back to the mill. She made her way into the city, a heavy bag of flour on her shoulder. No one suspected the quiet Quaker woman of anything more than purchasing a bag of flour for her family.

Message Delivered

As for William, "he little knew the part his wife had played in the drama of that eventful night. She feared the least suspicion of his having taken information out of the city might endanger his life and kept her secret."[5] That evening Lydia shuddered while sitting by her window as she observed the British troops march out to town on their way to attack Washington's men.

The next day, Lydia went about her household duties praying her message had arrived on time. Shortly after the British troops returned, there was a knock on Lydia's door. When she opened it, an officer informed Lydia that Major Andre had summoned her to come to the council room. The Major locked the door behind her and told her to take a seat. The room was dark and helped to hide her pale, nervous face. Andre asked Lydia grimly if any of her family members had been awake on the night of their last council meeting. She replied, "No, indeed, they were all in bed at eight o'clock as thee bade me," she truthfully replied.[6]

The British officer, looking quite perplexed, explained, "I cannot understand it. It is very strange. I know that you were sound asleep for I had to knock several times on your door to awaken you to let us out. Yet it is certain that we were betrayed. I am entirely at a loss to imagine who gave General Washington information of our intended attack. On arrival near his encampment, we found his cannon mounted, the troops under arms and prepared at every point to meet us, and we have been compelled to march back like a parcel of fools. The walls must have ears."[7]

Instead of finding a sleeping camp, the British were attacked by the Pennsylvania militia which confused them. It was clear they would not have an easy victory as anticipated. After making a few half-hearted assaults, they abandoned the mission and marched back to Philadelphia, their headquarters, knowing their well-laid plans must have been betrayed.

What's in the Buttons?

This was not the only time Lydia helped supply information to Washington's army. Her location in town, the fact that she was a known peace-loving Quaker, and the frequent use of her council room by the British all contributed to her hearing plans of the enemy. She was also easily able to observe troop movements within the city. She often brought the officers refreshments while they met in her council room, or she would step into the room to add wood to the fire.

She devised an **ingenious** plan to transmit gained intelligence to her son Charles, in Washington's army. Her husband William had developed a secret code which he shared with Lydia and Charles. When Lydia obtained **intel**, William would write them in his code on scraps of paper. Lydia, who sewed clothes for her family, would **conceal** these messages in a cloth-covered button. Covered buttons were made of either metal or wood. Fabric covered the forms with a separate back piece that secured the fabric behind the button. The cover was generally the same fabric from which the coat was made. They were common and are still used by some people today.

ingenious: Clever

conceal: Hide

intel: Information

The message secured; the button was then sewed in place on the coat to be worn. William and Lydia had another son, John, who was 14 years old at the time. He was too young to join the Continental army, but he performed a valuable service to them in another way. Lydia would cut the buttons off John's coat, secure the messages safely inside his button covers, sew the buttons back on his coat, and send John off to Washington's camp where he would ask to speak to his brother Charles.

Charles would take John into his tent, remove his buttons, **decipher** the messages, and sew the buttons back onto his coat until the next time. Because he was a child, John was permitted to pass and repass the **sentries** without being stopped. It was an amazing plan. It wasn't until years later that Lydia revealed her valuable role in providing intelligence. If Lydia hadn't informed Washington of the British plans on so many occasions, the founding of America may have had a very different outcome.

decipher: Decode

sentries: Guards

Washington's Spies – The Culper Ring

1778–1783	Setauket, Long Island, New York

The Cause of the Conflict

The **French and Indian War** had cost Britain a great deal of money. King George and Parliament felt that since the money had been spent to defend the colonies, the colonies must now help pay for it. In 1765, Parliament authorized the Stamp Act, the first of many new and **oppressive** taxes. The colonists, and even some members of Parliament, opposed these taxes. They declared it was not right for the colonies to have to bear the tax burden when they had no representation in Parliament and therefore couldn't vote on the **implementation** of these taxes. Thus began the struggle of the Patriot colonists against King George's oppression.

French and Indian War: War between French, Indians, and British for territory in the Ohio Valley

oppressive: Unjust hardship

implementation: Putting into use

Continentals: Patriot colonists

Some of the colonists supported King George and were called Tories or Loyalists. Those who opposed the king were called **Continentals**. The Patriots appealed for fair representation in parliament but were turned down on multiple occasions. They were further burdened with such things as British troops being **quartered** in their own homes. At last, they concluded that they must fight for their freedom.

quartered: British soldiers living in colonists' homes without colonists' consent

Second Continental Congress: Colonial delegates that formally met to decide issues of independence

intelligence: Information about the enemy

Commander-in-Chief

During the **Second Continental Congress**, George Washington was chosen as Commander-in-Chief of the Continental army. On July 3, 1775, Washington took charge of the newly-formed army — only about 15,000 men with little ammunition or supplies. It was an almost impossible idea to think of defeating the most powerful army in the world at the time with so little in the way of resources or manpower. Washington knew it would be only through obtaining better **intelligence** that the Continentals would stand any chance at all. This was a big lesson he learned from fighting in the French and Indian War. "There is nothing more necessary than good Intelligence to frustrate a designing enemy, & nothing that requires greater pains to obtain."[8] On July 15, 1775, only weeks after taking charge, he paid about $333.33 in gold to an unidentified person to "go into the town of Boston to establish a secret correspondence for the purpose of **conveying** intelligence of the Enemy's movements and **designs**. (That was a large payment: $333.33 in 1775 would buy about what $7600.00 would buy today.)"[9]

Establishment of the Culper Ring

Many men and women tried to gather information about the enemy. One such effort was made by Nathan Hale, who lost his life in the attempt. Washington did not want to see this happen again. More **safeguards** had to be put in place. George Washington chose Benjamin Tallmadge, an army officer who had been a close friend of Nathan Hale, to be in charge of a ring of **civilian** spies. Tallmadge, by August 1776, had achieved the rank of Captain of the 1st Troop of the **Second Dragoons**. He thus had impressed Washington with his trustworthiness and skill.

At this time, most of the information Washington needed was going to be found in New York, the location of the British army headquarters. Washington told Tallmadge he needed to know the size and location of British supplies, how many **cavalry** the British had, how much gunpowder they had in store, where the next attack might be planned, and how large each section of the British army was. Washington wanted the spy work to be carried out by men who knew the land, the water, and the people, in other words — local people.

conveying: Gathering and reporting

designs: Plans

safeguards: Measures taken to protect someone

civilian: Non-military

Second Dragoons: Elite force of troops on horseback

cavalry: Soldiers on horseback

Trusted Friends

Tallmadge had been born on Long Island, which was occupied at the time by the British. He began to set up his spy network by using trusted friends he had grown up with and who still lived in the area around Setauket on the Long Island Sound. They would make up the secretive Culper Ring. One such friend was Abraham Woodhull. Woodhull agreed to help, and thus the groundwork was laid for the spy ring to begin its work.

Tallmadge assigned Woodhull the code name Samuel Culper or Culper Sr. In this successful spy ring, the members didn't know who the other members (agents) were. They only knew the one to whom they were directly passing information. That way, if one member were caught, he didn't know anything that could **implicate** the others. This protection helped to make the agents more willing to take the risk. Washington himself didn't know who many of the agents were until years later. Tallmadge (code name John Bolton) would tell Washington what the agents discovered but not their true identities.

Woodhull was a farmer who, when both his brothers died, had taken on the responsibility of supporting his sister and aging parents. He didn't have any strong feelings about the war until his older cousin Nathaniel Woodhull was captured after the Battle of Long Island and soon died due to the harsh treatment he received in the British prison. Tallmadge

implicate: Expose

explained Washington's assignment to Woodhull. He was to set up a spy ring to convey information obtained from New York across the sound to Long Island, and from there to more **rural** areas of Connecticut. There, Tallmadge would be responsible for taking the sensitive information to wherever Washington was encamped at the time.

rural: Country rather than city

The Ring Grows

Woodhull immediately decided to approach his long-time friend Caleb Brewster, a blacksmith and physically strong boatman who knew every cove and waterway. Caleb liked adventurous challenges. When he was 19, Brewster had joined a whaleboat crew headed for Greenland. After that, he sailed on a merchant ship to London. When he returned to the colonies, the War of Independence was well underway, and Brewster promptly joined the fight for freedom. He began piloting small whaleboats through the British-controlled waters of the sound in the dark of night, obtaining and reporting enemy movements to Washington that he had observed firsthand. Brewster enthusiastically agreed to ferry messages to Connecticut. The British mistakenly thought Woodhull was a Loyalist farmer. Because of that, he knew he had to avoid all contact with Brewster. They needed to figure out how to transfer their messages without creating **suspicion**. So, Woodhull, under direction from Benjamin Tallmadge, approached another longtime friend and neighbor, Anna Strong, to help. Anna could see Woodhull's farm from her clothesline at the **ridge** of her property across a small bay. She also had a **birds-eye view** of all the coves. When Anna hung a black petticoat on her clothesline, it was a signal to Abraham Woodhull that Caleb Brewster had arrived in his whaleboat. The number of handkerchiefs she hung next to the black petticoat corresponded to one of the six coves that Brewster numbered for identification purposes. This told Woodhull in exactly which cove Brewster was hiding.

suspicion: Distrust

ridge: Top

birds-eye view: View from above

Then at night, Woodhull would deliver his message to Brewster directly, without having to risk being caught by the British, and without taking unnecessary time to locate the right cove by trial and error. Still under cover of darkness, Brewster would sail past British guard boats, crossing Long Island Sound to Fairfield, Connecticut. From Fairfield, a **courier** on a fast horse would relay the message to Tallmadge who quickly delivered it to Washington.

courier: Messenger

How the Ring Works

It wasn't long before Woodhull realized that he needed others in the spy ring to retrieve information from New York and save him from having to make so many trips himself, risking detection. He had a sister, Mary, who had married Amos Underhill. The couple lived in Manhattan, New York. Amos ran a boarding house where Woodhull stayed when he was in New York, but it would be suspicious if he was found making too many trips there. So, again, he turned to more of his trusted childhood friends.

Austin Roe owned a tavern in East Setauket that was **patronized** by British soldiers and Loyalists. He often overheard the enemy's conversations there. He had grown up with Caleb Brewster. As a tavern owner, he already had to make regular trips to New York for supplies. He became a willing courier. When British Redcoat sentries stopped him, he would say he was picking up supplies for his business, which was true.

patronized: Frequently visited for business

One of Roe's suppliers for goods who lived in New York was Robert Townsend (code name Samuel Culper Jr.). Robert's family owned a home and business on Oyster Bay, Long Island. Robert had tried to stay neutral until a company of the King's **Royal Rangers** led by Colonel John Simcoe, took possession of the Townsend family home for their headquarters, allowing the family to use only a few back rooms.

Royal Rangers: Loyalist military unit of the American Revolutionary War

The Rangers treated the home carelessly, and at Simcoe's order, destroyed the vast apple orchard that Robert's father had tended diligently for years. The British troops ate all the apples and cut down all the trees to keep British fires burning. Certain freedoms in the town were taken away, properties were destroyed, and Simcoe did not allow residents to protest or appeal.

Townsend owned a dry goods store in Manhattan. The seaport town was close to Amos Underhill's boarding house. Townsend supplied both Loyalists and British commanders at his store and consequently heard much information in a business day. While checking on his shipments at the docks, he could easily observe ship and troop movements as well. Townsend had the perfect cover to be a spy.

Just a few blocks from Townsend's store were James Rivington's print shop and coffee house. Rivington was an outspoken Loyalist. His newspaper boldly supported King George. Townsend came up with a plan to gather even more enemy secrets. He volunteered to write a column for Rivington's paper, reporting local news. Now Culper Jr. (Townsend) was a reporter for the Loyalist newspaper! Loyalists and the British would actually expect him to ask them about the movement of troops and supplies into and out of the city. At Rivington's coffee house, he would regularly meet British officers, gathering crucial information.

Roe, after receiving intelligence reports from Townsend, would ride back to Long Island. He would place his report in a box buried on Woodhull's farm. This kept him from having to make direct contact with Woodhull. After recovering the report, Woodhull would take out his telescope and look across the bay to Anna Strong's clothesline to determine where to deliver it to Brewster. The entire process to get a message to Washington took about two weeks.

The spy ring grew. It developed efficient ways to deliver information more rapidly and protect its agents better. Along with a code name, each agent was assigned a number for security purposes. This also made it easier to write messages. Benjamin Tallmadge was agent 721; Abraham Woodhull was agent 722; Caleb Brewster, agent 725; Anna Strong was believed to be agent 355 (it's possible this number referred to multiple women during the war because 355 was a code number for the word 'lady'). Austin Roe was courier agent 724; Robert Townsend, agent 723; and George Washington was agent 711.

Secret Messages

Benjamin Tallmadge, now promoted to the rank of Major, invented a secret code for writing communications. He substituted digits for words he used. He made only four copies of his codes, one for himself, one for Woodhull, one for Townsend, and one for General Washington. All his agents received a **cipher**. An agent's real name was never used in a message, only his number or code name.

All messages were written using a newly developed special ink. It consisted of two different chemicals — one to write the message, the other to be brushed over the written message to make it visible. This two-bottle system was much more secure. It was just what General Washington needed. Washington gave special instructions for how agents were to use this system: "He should occasionally write his information on the blank sleeves of a pamphlet... a common book, or on the blank leaves at each end of registers, almanacs, or any new publication or book of small value. A much better way is to write a letter with some mixture of family matters between the lines on the remaining part of the sheet."[10]

cipher: Each letter in a message is replaced by another letter or number

The Culper Ring was extremely successful. Time and again it provided Washington with essential intelligence. They uncovered a British plot to

print counterfeit colonial money, making Continental dollars decrease in value. That would have hurt the Patriot cause tremendously. They also helped to uncover the **traitorous** plan of Benedict Arnold to turn over West Point fort to the British. If that had happened, the war would have ended with a British victory. Time-sensitive information received from the Culper Ring enabled Washington to secure the safe arrival of French reinforcements and avoid a British attack.

Somehow Rivington managed to get a copy of the entire British naval codebook, which was more than Tallmadge could have dared hope for. The siege of Yorktown was an overwhelming success due partly to obtaining this codebook.

traitorous: Disloyal

The war was drawing to a close. "After five years, four major plots thwarted, countless misgivings, close calls and untold sleepless nights, the Culper correspondence came to an end."[11] In the words of Major George Beckwith, British Intelligence Officer, "Washington did not really outfight the British, he simply outspied us."[12]

Anna Strong – Petticoat Spy

1778–1783	Setauket, Long Island, New York

War of Independence

George Washington had just managed to drive the British troops out of Boston after **fortifying** Dorchester Heights. Washington knew the British would now focus their efforts on New York. New York Harbor was the main supply line between the northern and southern colonies — for men, supplies, and transportation. If the British could gain control of this busy waterway, they would stand a good chance of winning the entire war. The British were sending thousands of troops into New York Harbor. Washington was outnumbered and under-supplied with ammunition. Mostly what he needed, though, was knowledge of the enemy's plans. During his involvement in the French and Indian War, Washington had learned that a war was not won through might but through intelligence. What he needed most were spies.

fortifying: Strengthening

Born and Raised in Long Island

Nancy (commonly known as Anna) Smith was born on April 14, 1740, in the house her great-grandfather had built when he first arrived in the colonies. When she was 20 years old, she married Selah Strong, a judge in the colonies, and began to raise a family in Setauket, Long

Island. Their home was one of Long Island's **manors** on Strong's Neck. Many of Anna's relatives were Tories but Anna and Selah were **Patriots**. Selah was a **delegate** to the first three provincial congresses in colonial New York, and in 1776, was a captain in the New York **militia**. He was one of the Minutemen whose job it was to be ready at a minute's notice to defend and protect the colonies. Many of the Minutemen were led by their pastors and would gather on the **Village Green** after church to practice military drills in order to be prepared.

The political position Anna's husband held soon made him a **target** of the British soldiers who were occupying the Long Island area of New York. The **Redcoats** turned the Presbyterian Church on the Village Green into a fort, destroying the church pews to make room for their horses and pulling up tombstones from the church graveyard to use for **barricades**.

The Battle of Setauket had previously taken place on August 22, 1777, when a fleet of Patriot whaleboats arrived from Connecticut but failed to take over the fort. Selah Strong was soon arrested for "surreptitious correspondence with the enemy."[13] That meant the British thought he was a spy. In a short

manors: Large country house with lands

Patriots: Supporters of the colonies' rights

delegate: Elected official sent to represent others

militia: Groups of men who protected their communities

Village Green: Area in center of town used for community events

target: Person selected as the aim of an attack

Redcoats: British soldiers so called because of their red military jackets

barricades: Objects lined up to prevent troops from getting past them

time, Anna learned he was being held on the prison ship *Jersey* which was docked in **Wallabout Bay**. The Patriots lost more men from the bad treatment and starvation they endured on that ship than those who died in battle. The ship housed around 1,000 prisoners at one time. Yellow fever was prevalent on the ship, as was smallpox. It is estimated that 11,000 men died while imprisoned there.

Anna and her Children Must Move

Soon after Selah was taken prisoner, the British troops told Anna that she must leave her grand manor house on Strong's Neck. Its location overlooking Long Island Sound, which lay across the bay from Connecticut, provided a perfect location for the British to set up base. Anna moved to a small cottage on her large estate. Empty homes suffered greater destruction; by staying on her property, she hoped to ensure it would not be subject to harm. Many women did this during the Revolution, as they were not viewed by the British as dangerous. Also, Anna thought she might be able to hear

Wallabout Bay:
Small body of water-later known as the Brooklyn Navy Yard

important information to pass along to the Patriots since she was in a perfect **strategic** position to assist the Setauket spies.

Selah Is Released

Anna begged help from her Tory relatives to try to obtain Selah's release from the dark hold of the prison ship. She was allowed to bring him food and she brought plenty for the British soldiers as well. It's believed Selah finally was released in exchange for food, plus persuasion from Anna's influential relatives. Although he was set free, Selah could not be sure he would be safe from the British. He fled to Connecticut, which was still held by the Patriots, for the remainder of the war, taking with him some of their younger children. This gave Anna more time to become a vital link in the Patriots' cause.

strategic: Carefully designed to achieve military advantage

Becoming a Spy

Travel between Long Island and New York City was becoming increasingly dangerous. Anyone on this route might be stopped, searched, robbed, or even attacked without warning. George Washington desperately needed a way to get information about

the British plans, troop locations, and supply routes. He recognized that without this information the war would be lost. So, he chose a man to set up a network of spies code-named the Culper Ring to carry information on a complex route from New York City to Setauket, across Long Island Sound to Fairfield, Connecticut, and finally to him. It was named after Culpeper, Virginia, the county where young Washington had been a surveyor at the age of 17. The ring consisted mostly of childhood friends who had grown up on Long Island and were therefore very familiar with the countryside. It was kept so secretive that even George Washington didn't know the members of the spy network till many years later. Anna was **recruited** by Major Benjamin Tallmadge from Setauket. He was the main ringleader. Anna had known him since childhood. Thus, Anna became the first female spy in the Culper Spy Ring.

recruited: Asked to join

How the Spy Ring Worked

Every week one of the spies rode to New York City to collect information about the British troops. Abraham Woodhull was one of them. He was Anna Strong's neighbor who lived across the bay. Anna made the trip to New York City at least once with him, pretending to be his wife. A letter from Abraham Woodhull to Major Tallmadge on August 15, 1779, reads, "I intend to visit 727 (code for New York) before long and think by the assistance of a 355 (code for lady) of my acquaintance shall be able to outwit them all."[14] Usually, though, this was too dangerous to be necessary. Another spy normally made the trip and when he returned, he would hide a message in a wooden box that was kept buried on Abraham Woodhull's farm. Another spy and friend, Caleb Brewster, had been a whaleboat captain and therefore knew Long Island Sound well. Slipping past the British he would hide in one of the many coves in the bay. Brewster had assigned a number to each one of the coves. When Anna stood on the bluff of Strong's Neck, she had a clear view not only of Long Island Sound, but also six different coves, three on each side of the point.

The Spy with a Clothesline

That's where Anna's clothesline came in. Once she saw which cove Brewster was hiding in, she would go to her clothesline and begin to hang out clothes. A black **petticoat** signaled that a message was waiting to be delivered to General Washington. Then she would carefully hang handkerchiefs next to the petticoat. The number of handkerchiefs

petticoat: Garment worn under a dress for extra warmth

revealed which cove Brewster was waiting in. That way, Abraham Woodhull knew exactly where to find Caleb Brewster instead of fumbling around from cove to cove in search of him. If she observed that the British were near any one of the coves, she would hang a red petticoat on the line, with handkerchiefs to alert him as to which cove, they were in so he would be sure to stay away from that one. Hidden by the darkness, Woodhull would sneak across his fields at night to meet Brewster in the same tidal marshes they had explored as children. With message in hand, Brewster would row to Fairfield, Connecticut, and deliver the message to the **spymaster** who then took it directly to General Washington. The British never suspected a woman hanging clothes on a clothesline had anything to do with delivering messages to their enemies.

spymaster: Head of an organization of spies

Invisible Ink

The messages were written in a special code the spymaster had devised. He called it the "numerical dictionary" because each number stood for a word. The ink used was invisible and made from a mixture of **ferrous sulfate** and water. When received, the paper was placed over a candle flame to reveal the message. If available, a chemical called sodium carbonate could be rubbed over the message to reveal the hidden words instead of

ferrous sulfate: Green iron salt

using candle flames. The ink had been invented before the war by a physician named James Jay, brother of the well-known Patriot leader John Jay, who later became the first chief justice of the newly formed United States Supreme Court.

Now, even if a spy were stopped and searched, there would be nothing to find. In addition, Washington suggested that a good place to write messages would be between the lines of a book or publication so as not to create suspicion.

Each spy was assigned a unique number to identify him. Anna may have had the code name agent 355, which was the code word for lady. There were other ladies listening and reporting information to the ring but because of the secrecy of the mission, it's not known if this was just Anna's number or if it meant any of the women helping. This messaging system worked perfectly throughout the war. A steady stream of intelligence was delivered, and critical information was supplied by the Culper spies that proved instrumental in helping to reveal Benedict Arnold's traitorous plan to give up the American fort at West Point to the British.

After the War

After the war, Anna was reunited with her husband Selah and the children he had taken with him to safety in Connecticut. They moved back into their large manor house which had survived the war safely. They lived there with their eight children, Keturah (born 1761), Thomas (born 1765), Margaret (born 1768), Benjamin (born 1770), Mary (who died young), William (born 1775), Joseph (born 1777), and their son born after the war whom they named George Washington Strong (born 1783). It is thought that Thomas may have helped his mother occasionally by taking trips to the bay to see if Caleb Brewster was waiting in one of the coves or to check on the presence of Redcoats in the area.

A Visit from President Washington

In April 1790, George Washington who had been elected the first President of the newly established country, came to Long Island. He visited the Culper spies to extend his deepest thanks for courageously risking their lives during the war, although he may not have known all the details of how it was accomplished, such as the use of the clothesline. At the time, Selah and Anna's grandson, Selah B. Strong, who helped to entertain President Washington, did not know that his grandparents had been a vital part of the spy ring. The identities of these spies were kept a secret for over 150 years. Historian Morton Pennypacker found old letters in a trunk in the attic of the Townsend family home (Robert Townsend had been one of the spies in the chain). He figured out the code and in 1939 published his findings in his book, *George Washington's Spies on Long Island and in New York.*

If you have the opportunity to visit Long Island, New York, you can see the Village Green in Setauket, the Presbyterian Church, and Strong's Neck where the spy activities took place. The Three Village Historical Society in East Setauket has much information about the famous spy ring. Raynham Hall is now a museum open to the public.

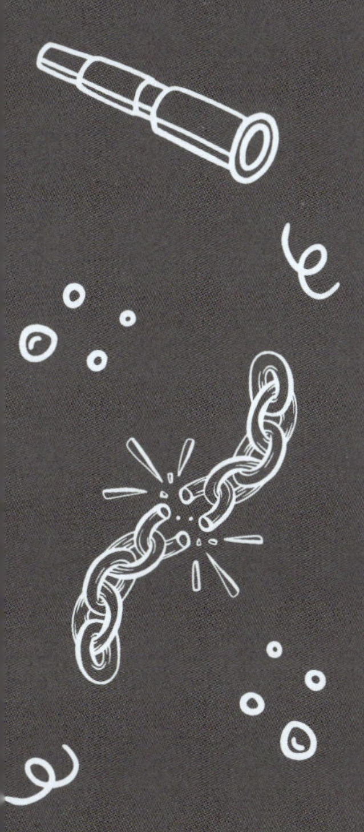

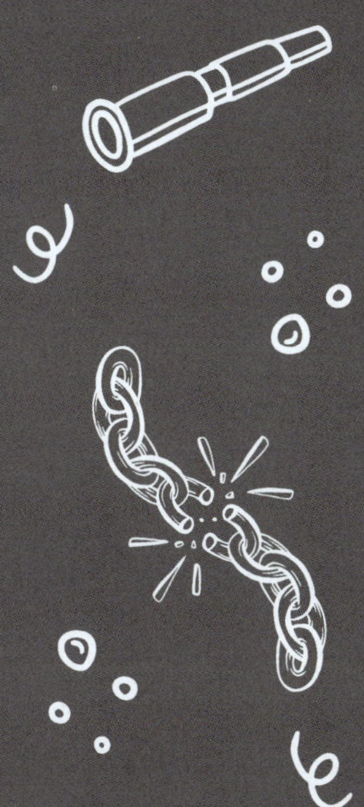

5

James Armistead Lafayette—Double Spy

1781	Williamsburg — Yorktown, Virginia

War of Independence

At least 5,000 African American men served with the Patriot army during the seven-year-long War of Independence. When the war began, only two and a half million people lived in the colonies; one-half million of those were African American. By the end of the war, 60,000 slaves who had fought to help win freedom for the nation were now set free. This story is about one of those without whom the American army may have never achieved victory.

Marquis de Lafayette

The Marquis de Lafayette, one of the richest men in France at the time, was only 19 years old when he listened to the Duke of Gloucester, brother of King George III, speak mockingly about the colonists wanting the right to govern themselves. "My heart was enlisted," he later confessed in his memoirs, "and I thought only of joining my colors to those of the revolutionaries."[15] He secretly set sail for America and once here, endeared himself to General George Washington, who soon made Lafayette his information officer. It was Lafayette's job to gather intelligence for the army. He set out to recruit spies from all walks of life and sent them undercover behind British lines. By the summer of 1781, the primary location of the war had moved to the southern colonies of Georgia, South Carolina, and North Carolina and Virginia.

James Armistead Joins the Army

James Armistead was a slave of William Armistead of Williamsburg. He was only 21 years old, when he heard that Lafayette was coming through town to recruit black men to serve in the Continental army. Armistead was very interested. He could read and write, unlike many other slaves, and this skill earned him the position of handling the clerical work and running the household for his master. A devoted Patriot himself, his master permitted Armistead to leave with Lafayette but wanted him to return when the war was over.

Lafayette recognized Armistead's qualities and abilities at once, and expected he would be loyal and valuable to the American cause. Lafayette decided that Armistead would be a spy, not a soldier. The fact that he was a slave ensured that the British would not suspect him. Britain had offered black colonists' freedom if they joined the British cause, and hundreds of black men took them up on the offer.

Armistead's first assignment was to the camp of Benedict Arnold, posing as a slave escaping from the American Patriots. His mission was to relay information back to Lafayette. The British never suspected the pleasant black man who so willingly made himself their servant in camp and guide on the roads that he knew so well. Armistead took note of the number of cannon and British troop positions. He listened to groups of soldiers when they spoke of the war. He wanted to understand how the soldiers felt about the war to determine their

morale, and to estimate how many soldiers were on the move. He waited on tables as officers discussed strategy, objectives, and plans of attack. Nobody tried to hide information from an escaped slave.

Armistead sent messengers back almost daily to Lafayette with the valuable information he had learned. When Benedict Arnold left Virginia, Armistead was reassigned to the camp of Lord Cornwallis, where he served as a waiter at the headquarters. Cornwallis was very guarded with information, but Armistead still sent regular reports to Lafayette. He most likely stood near the general while he ate his meals and could overhear the officers' conversations.

morale: General mood among the soldiers

Lafayette Expresses Concern

Lafayette reported to Washington on July 9, 1781, "This Cornwallis is much wiser than the other generals with whom I have dealt. He inspires me with a sincere fear, and his name has greatly troubled my sleep. This campaign is a good school for me. God grant that the public does not pay for my lessons."[16] Although fearful of Cornwallis,

Lafayette continued to camp close by, so he was available to receive the messages of Redcoat movements from Armistead.

In July, Cornwallis' army moved east and set up camp in the town of Portsmouth, near Chesapeake Bay. Armistead sent a report to Lafayette that a fleet of sailing ships had arrived in the harbor, but they sat idle in the bay for weeks. The enemy troops remained in camp at Portsmouth. At last, in early August, the Redcoats left Portsmouth in their ships.

One day as Armistead was traveling through the countryside between American lines and British headquarters, he noticed signs of massive numbers of troops on the move. The British Navy began landing ten thousand British soldiers in the vicinity of Yorktown. Armistead knew this meant a major operation was being planned. Quickly, he passed the information along to Lafayette, who in turn got word to Washington. Washington acted quickly, hoping to trap the British. Yorktown, a small tobacco port on the York River, was the place Cornwallis had chosen for his headquarters. Lafayette moved his troops to Williamsburg, to keep a close watch on the British. It was steamy, hot weather, and Cornwallis did not seem to be in a hurry to build defenses around the city.

Double Spy

It was about this time that James Armistead himself reported back to Lafayette with the news that Cornwallis had sent him there as a spy for the British! He was now a double spy. He would deliver

disinformation prepared by Lafayette to Cornwallis, all the while informing Lafayette of Cornwallis' movements and plans. Armistead knew he was taking huge risks but found it fairly easy to fool Cornwallis. If caught, though, he knew he would face death.

The French had pledged their vital support to help the Americans gain independence earlier in February. Washington now informed Lafayette of some exciting news he had just received. On July 28, French Commander De Grasse wrote to General Washington that, "the whole will be embarked in vessels of war from twenty-five to twenty-nine in number, which will depart from this colony (West Indies) on the 3rd of August and proceed directly to the Chesapeake Bay."[17]

disinformation: Inaccurate data

Preparing for Battle and Victory

Washington and the French commander in America, **Count** Rochambeau, were on the march with their troops at the same time the French fleets were sailing toward the Chesapeake. The French fleet was comprised of 24 ships, armed with a total of 19,000 sailors and 1,700 guns. The smaller British fleet at the time consisted of only 19 ships, with 13,000 sailors and 1,400 guns

count: Military commander

total. Washington planned to cut the British off by both land and sea. He gave orders for Lafayette to keep Cornwallis in Yorktown to prevent his army from escaping. Lafayette wrote to Washington, "I hope you will find we have taken the best precautions to lessen his Lordship's chances to escape."[18]

By mid-September, Washington's and Rochambeau's troops began arriving at Williamsburg where they were welcomed by Lafayette. Two weeks later, they marched the few miles to Yorktown, led by Lafayette's small **regiment**, and began digging trenches. The French brought in huge cannons and in early October, the firing began. The French fleet had the British hemmed in at Chesapeake Bay. The American and French soldiers had them trapped by land. Cornwallis knew that if reinforcements didn't arrive in time from New York, his trapped army would not be able to withstand the siege from the French and Americans. After only 10 days of fighting, Cornwallis and his troops surrendered. Cornwallis felt so defeated that he didn't even attend the official surrender when his men laid down their arms.

regiment: Large group of soldiers divided into various units

Armistead's Service Is Recognized

A couple of days later when Cornwallis went to Lafayette's headquarters to make arrangements, he was shocked to see James Armistead standing by Lafayette's side wearing the uniform of a Continental soldier. It was only then that he realized the volunteer who had served him so faithfully was actually a double spy, working for the Americans. James Armistead's loyal service as a double agent was instrumental in achieving this great victory. This was recognized by Lafayette after the war had ended.

Wanting to help Armistead obtain freedom from slavery, he wrote to him, praising his dangerous work as a spy.

> "This is to certify that the Bearer By the Name of James Has done Essential Services to me While I Had the Honour to Command in this State. His Intelligences from the Enemy's Camp were Industriously Collected and More faithfully deliver'd. He properly Acquitted Himself with Some important Commissions I Gave Him and Appears to me Entitled to Every Reward his Situation Can Admit of. Done Under my Hand, Richmond November 21st, 1784. –Lafayette."[19]

Armistead sent this certificate to the General Assembly of Virginia and requested that he be declared a free man. He wrote concerning his service, "During the time of his serving the Marquis de Lafayette he often at the peril of his life found means to frequent the British camp, by which means he kept an open channel of the most useful communications to the army of the state . . . of the most secret & important kind; the possession of which if discovered on him would have most certainly endangered the life of your petitioner."[20] However, he would not accept that freedom unless his master William Armistead was paid a reasonable price for the loss of his trusted slave. The Assembly voted to pay Armistead a fair price, and from that time on, James called himself James Armistead Lafayette, in tribute to his friend the Marquis de Lafayette, who had done so much to help him obtain his freedom.

After the War

James Lafayette married and raised a large family. He purchased 40 acres of farmland near the estate of his former master, whom he considered a friend. In 1819, when he was getting old and feeble, he again petitioned the General Assembly to request monetary help. They voted to give him about $60, a large sum at the time; also, he was to be given $40 per year for the remainder of his life, similar to **pensions** given to privates who had served in the army during the War of Independence.

pensions: Retirement money

A highlight in Armistead's life came in 1824, when America's dear friend the Marquis de Lafayette, who had risked his life for American freedom, returned to visit Richmond. He was now 64 years old; this would be the Marquis' last visit to America. Crowds lined up to honor this great French hero. When Lafayette recognized his old friend James Armistead Lafayette, he stopped and climbed off his horse to hug James, greeting him as an old **comrade** and friend.

Lafayette's friendship with Armistead may have influenced him to become a leader to end slavery in other countries including France. In Paris, he founded a society named The Friends of the Blacks, and for the remainder of his life, he helped to support efforts to give equal rights to men of all races.

comrade: Fellow soldier

James Armistead Lafayette died at the age of 72 in Virginia. A monument in Prospect Heights, New York, pictures the Marquis de Lafayette on his horse with James Armistead Lafayette at his side. James Armistead Lafayette is portrayed standing beside Lafayette and his horse in the famous painting by Jean-Baptiste Le Paon, featuring the surrender at Yorktown.

The Civil War

Tension had grown between the Northern and Southern states, leading to the Southern states seceding and forming the Confederate States of America. The war officially began when Confederate forces attacked Fort Sumter in 1861. The Northern states, known as the Union, and the Southern states engaged in a horrible and deadly conflict that affected the entire nation.

Key battles, such as Gettysburg and Antietam, played crucial roles in shaping the outcome of the war. President Abraham Lincoln, a strong advocate for preserving the Union, issued the Emancipation Proclamation in 1863, declaring all slaves in Confederate-held territories free. This move added a moral basis to the war.

The Union's victory in 1865 marked the end of the Civil War and the beginning of the Reconstruction era, aimed at rebuilding the country. The war had a profound impact on the nation, shaping its future and ultimately leading to the end of slavery.

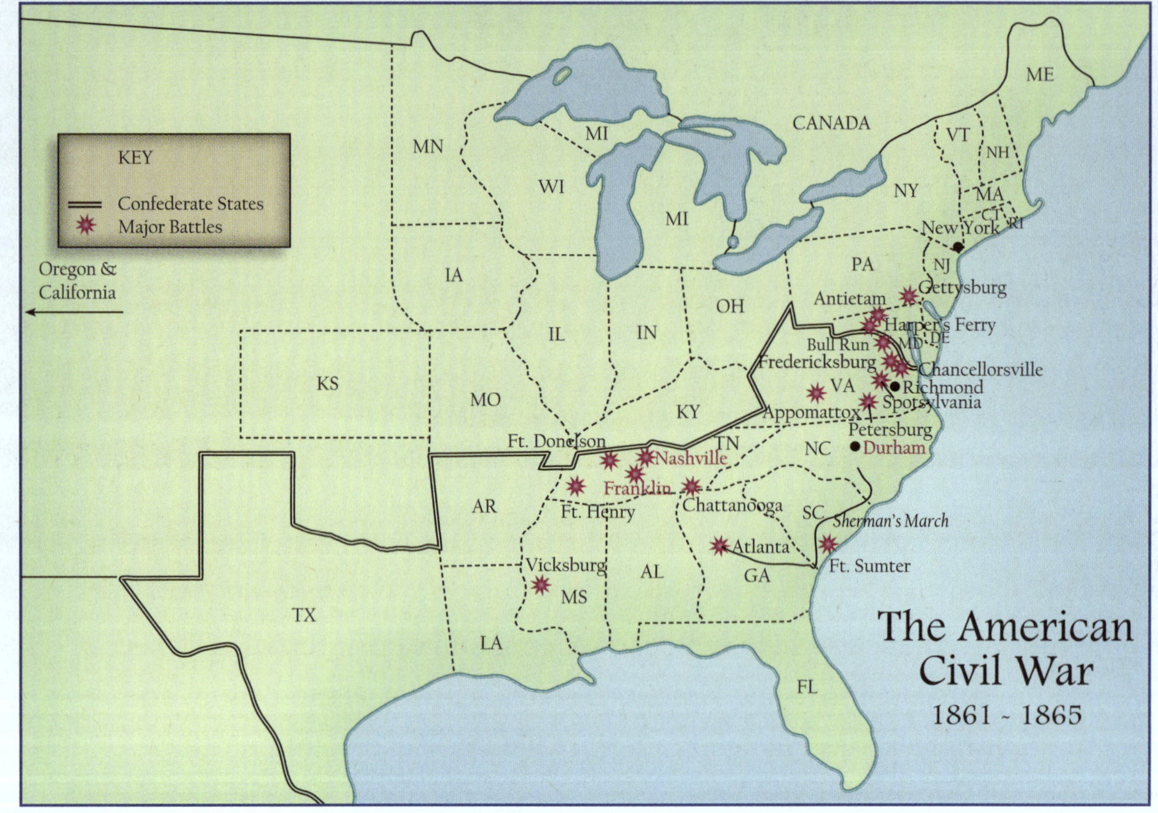

6

Belle Boyd – Teen-aged Spy

1861–1865	From Martinsburg, Virginia, to Front Royal, Virginia, to the Old Capitol Prison in Washington D.C.

The frame of mind for most Southerners when the Civil War was on the horizon must be explained to appreciate Belle's story. To Southerners at the time, the major issue for which they were willing to fight was the right of the states to govern themselves as outlined in the Constitution and just as important for some was also their right to own slaves, which had been a contentious argument since the country was formed. Slavery was abolished by northern states, yet was legalized by the southern states as slaves were needed to grow and harvest crops. Southerners believed the Federal government was overstepping its bounds and therefore felt obligated to defend their freedom before they lost any more of their rights; and for those with slaves, that included the right to own them. It was not an issue they took lightly.

Growing-up Years

Belle Boyd was born on May 9, 1844, in the pretty little village of Martinsburg, Virginia, in the Shenandoah Mountains. She had a love for horses and as a child, spent many hours on horseback exploring her beloved Shenandoah Valley. At the age of 12, she attended Mount Washington College in Baltimore, Maryland, and completed her education there at age 16. Upon graduating, Belle spent fun, happy hours socializing in Washington, D.C. However, life was about to change drastically for Belle. A civil war was brewing. Belle believed that the rights of states were at stake, and the choice of which side to take was easy for Belle. Her place was no longer in Washington, and she left immediately for her Valley.

War Comes to the Valley

When Belle's state of Virginia decided to secede from the Union, men from every village and town volunteered to answer the call to arms. Belle's father was one of the first to volunteer. He was assigned to the 2nd Virginian Regiment, which later belonged to the section of the Confederate army known as **"The Stonewall Brigade."** Money for arms and equipment for this regiment was raised by the women, and Belle was one of those heading up the fundraising drive.

It was on July 4th, the 85th anniversary of the signing of the Declaration of Independence, that the noise of soldiers was heard in the streets of Martinsburg. A group of quarrelsome, rowdy **Yankees** soldiers began to enter citizens' homes forcibly, destroying personal property, firing shots, and **pillaging**.

The Stonewall Brigade: Famous combat unit led by General Thomas 'Stonewall' Jackson

Yankees: Confederate word for Union soldiers

pillaging: Stealing

The Boyd home was not left untouched. The Yankees, trying to stir up strife, then decided to raise a Union flag over the house to signify the occupants were in agreement with the Federal cause. At this, Belle's mother stepped forward and quietly proclaimed, "Men, every member of my household will die before that flag shall be raised over us."[21]

One of the soldiers began insulting and threatening Mrs. Boyd. Belle, sensing that her mother's life was in real danger, drew her pistol and fired at him. The soldiers left the house hurriedly but proceeded to pile up hay to set the house on fire. A messenger reported the trouble to the nearby Federal headquarters and an officer came to investigate. Thankfully, he arrived before the fire was lit. The Federal officer concluded, on questioning all involved, that Belle Boyd "had done perfectly right."[22] He stationed sentries around the house to protect the family from further mischief by unruly soldiers.

Gathering Information

Because of the daily presence of Federal officers, Belle was able to collect much information about the position and plans of the enemy, which she then began to send in secret messages to one of the Confederate officers in the area. However, somehow one of these notes fell into enemy hands and Belle's handwriting was identified. An 'Article of War' was delivered to her as a warning. It stated, "Whoever shall give food, ammunition to, or aid and abet the enemies of the United States Government in any manner whatever, shall suffer death, or whatever the penalty the honourable members of the Court-martial shall see fit to inflict."[23] Little did they know that Belle had already been **confiscating** Yankee pistols and swords from officers and taking them to the Confederate camp. From then on, Belle was watched very carefully.

After the Confederate victory at the Battle of Bull Run, Belle was visiting her uncle and aunt in the picturesque village of Front Royal, Virginia. They had previously lived in Washington but fled the Northern capital when their strong Southern **sympathies** became known. The Yankee soldiers then confiscated their magnificent home and **converted** it into **barracks** for soldiers. Front Royal was chosen as the site for a large hospital to care for many of the Confederate soldiers who had been wounded in the Battle of Bull Run. Belle, wanting to do all she could for her country's cause, joined in and spent the next eight weeks in **incessant** nursing. When her health began to suffer, she was forced to return to her home in Martinsburg to recover under her mother's care.

confiscating: Secretly taking

sympathies: Feelings

converted: Changed

barracks: Living quarters

incessant: Non-stop

Interesting Encounters

When she was better, Belle and her mother made a trip to Manassas to visit her father for a few weeks. While there, she had the opportunity to be a courier between Confederate Generals Beauregard and Jackson. As courier, Belle was now an official member of the Confederate intelligence service, or more simply put, a spy. The winter passed quietly and Belle and her mother were hopeful that **reconciliation** might be made between the North and the South. Spring, however, proved that was not to be so.

Federal troops marched to Martinsburg again and captured it. Belle's father sent her back to Front Royal, hoping the location would be safer. Soon after, however, Front Royal was under attack again. Belle, worried about her mother at home, determined to go to check on her. She secured a pass and reached Winchester, Virginia, with no trouble. But here the Federal **Provost-Marshal** had her **detained** because someone reported that Belle might be a spy. Belle showed him her pass. Confused as to how to proceed, he decided to take her, along with other prisoners in his care, to Baltimore to hand her over to General Dix and let him decide her

reconciliation: Peace

Provost-Marshal: Union army officer in charge of maintaining order for soldiers and citizens

detained: Forced to stay

destiny. Belle spent a week in Baltimore and when General Dix could find no information against her, he released her to go home.

Under Suspicion

Back in Martinsburg, Belle was under great suspicion and forbidden to leave the village limits until finally, she obtained a pass from the local Provost-Marshal for herself and her mother to travel to Front Royal. Arriving there, they found the Federals had taken over the hotel which had been run by her cousin and grandmother, who were now living in the small cottage in the hotel courtyard. This cottage later became known as the "Belle Boyd cottage." Belle learned that a Federal council-of-war was to be held that night in the **drawing room** of the hotel. She crept to the bedroom directly above the drawing room to **eavesdrop**. She found a closet where someone had bored a hole in the floor, and putting her ear to the opening, she could easily hear the conversation. When it ended several hours later, she returned to her room in the cottage.

drawing room: Large room for entertaining

eavesdrop: Listen secretly

Here she quickly converted the information she had heard into a secret code. Grabbing a few passes she had previously obtained from **paroled** Confederate officers, she slipped out to the stable and saddled her horse, determined to deliver the message. Riding approximately 15 miles through the starless night she reached the home of a friend and knocked furiously on the door. She needed to see Colonel Ashby who was staying there!

Colonel Ashby had earned well his command in the Confederate army. Surprised, Colonel Ashby came out exclaiming, "Miss Belle, is this you? Where did you come from?"[24] Belle gave him the coded note and briefly told him what she had heard. Message delivered, Belle climbed on her horse and headed for Front Royal. When dawn broke, Belle was back in her bed fast asleep. The Confederates now knew the exact route the Federals planned to take and how they planned to trap General Jackson.

paroled: Released from duty

More Dispatches

Belle was quite creative both in discovering and delivering intelligence. On one occasion while near Winchester, she received an important dispatch to deliver to General Jackson, but she would need a pass to travel. She had a bouquet of flowers delivered to a Federal

Provost-Marshal with her compliments, requesting a pass to return to Front Royal. He, being flattered, thanked the dear lady for so sweet a compliment and granted her request.

At another time, Belle heard a commotion outside. She saw a Federal officer nearby and asked what was happening. He told her the Confederates were approaching and the Yankees were trying to get their supplies out of the city so the Confederates couldn't seize them. They planned to burn the bridges as soon as they crossed them. Belle realized that General Jackson was fast approaching and needed this valuable information. She tried to persuade some Southern men standing nearby to take it to him quickly. They all refused, claiming it was too dangerous. So Belle, without hesitating, raced to her horse and rode straight through the Yankee artillery lines into harm's way. **Crossfire** caused her to be thrown to the ground and shell fragments fell all around her, but she got up and kept going. "Fully aware now of the great peril into which her impetuous dash had carried her, fear and courage, the love of life and the steadfast determination to serve the cause of the South without faltering, fought their own battle within her."[25]

crossfire: Gunfire from two directions

A cheer went up from the First Maryland Regiment in tribute to the brave young girl as she raced valiantly to deliver her message. General Jackson, realizing the danger she had risked and the valuable nature of her message, rode forward and offered her an **escort** back to Front Royal. She was utterly exhausted when she arrived at Front Royal, but was delighted to see Confederate soldiers safely marching through the village, shouting their thanks to their heroine, Miss Belle Boyd. That evening, May 23, 1862, a note was delivered to her. It read, "Miss Belle Boyd, I thank you, for myself and for the army, for the immense service that you have rendered to your country today. Hastily, I am your friend, T. J. Jackson, C.S.A."[26]

escort: Guide for protection

Belle is Arrested

Not long after, Belle was betrayed by a Yankee spy posing as a paroled soldier headed South. She was arrested and escorted by a troop of 450 men because the Yankees were afraid Colonel Ashby's men would attempt to rescue Belle along the way. After making several failed attempts at escape, she ended up in the Old Capitol Prison in Washington, D.C. Here hundreds of persons were housed, "subjected to military arrest and detention without formal accusation or trial. ...That their constitutional civil rights were being violated was officially neither of concern nor consequence."[27]

The 18-year-old spy was met by Mr. Wood, Superintendent of the prison. He welcomed her, calling her the celebrated rebel spy and telling her he would try to make her as comfortable as he was able. He led her to Room 6, warning her to have no communication with other prisoners. Her room was furnished **scantily** with a washstand, a mirror, a bed, and a table and chairs.

Belle was visited by a representative of the War Department who encouraged her to take an oath of allegiance to the Union. Of course, she declined, even though it would have meant instant release from prison. Instead, she replied, "If it is a crime to love the South, its cause, and its President, then I am a criminal. I am in your power; do with me as you please. I fear you not. I would rather lie down in this prison and die, than leave it owing allegiance to such a government as yours."[28] Cries of "Bravo! Bravo!" rang out as the other prisoners hailed her response to the opportunity to renounce her loyalty to the South.

scantily: Simply

Superintendent Wood, although pledged to the

North, was a Virginian. He had a liking for Southerners. He especially liked Belle Boyd. He said she was the most enthusiastic rebel who ever came under his charge. He also made known that although she received large sums of money from her father, she used it generously to provide comfort for fellow prisoners, rather than for herself.

The Prisoners Communicate

One evening while reading her Bible, Belle heard a knock on the wall to her right and then the sound of a knife scooping out plaster. Soon the hole was big enough to pass rolled-up notes through and thus began correspondence between prisoners. One of the most creative ways to communicate was to wrap notes around marbles and roll them back and forth between rooms when the guards weren't looking. Belle was loved by all the prisoners, and many recalled tears coming to their eyes as they heard her sweetly singing rebel songs such as 'Maryland, my Maryland.' It encouraged others as they witnessed her **fervor** for the cause.

One day, great relief came unexpectedly. Mr. Wood arrived with good news: "All you rebels get ready! You are going to Dixie tomorrow and Miss Belle is going with you!"[29] It was an arranged prisoner exchange.

fervor: Great loyalty

Home again, Belle busied herself caring for the wounded from the

Battle of Gettysburg, Pennsylvania. It wasn't long, though, until Belle was captured at her home in Martinsburg and imprisoned again, this time in Carroll Prison. Once again, the prisoners managed to communicate with each other. It was during this imprisonment that she helped another prisoner escape. Belle suffered a long illness, so she was released and taken to Richmond, Virginia.

President of the Confederacy Jefferson Davis, asked Belle to carry Confederate **dispatches** to England. Belle agreed, knowing it was a hazardous mission since Southern ports were **blockaded** by Federal ships. The only vessels operating were blockade runners, privately owned vessels in partnership with the Confederacy who took the risk of sailing past Northern guns. She took on the **fictitious** name of Mrs. Lewis to protect her identity and departed. Although the runners hoped they had slipped by the blockaders, on the morning of Belle's 20th birthday, they were suddenly **pursued**. Belle rushed to destroy her dispatches, burning them in the ship's fires. Their ship was captured, and it was discovered that the famous spy Belle Boyd was aboard. In his report, a young Federal sailor wrote, "Two females, one named Belle Boyd, a spy for the Rebels. She was at the Battle of Fredericksburg,

dispatches: Important written messages

blockaded: Sealed off

fictitious: Pretended

pursued: Chased

encouraging the soldiers and giving the Rebel General a great deal of information with regard to how our armies were situated, and it was she who won the battle of Bull Run. This makes the 4th time she has been captured and what they will do with her I do not know. I guess they will keep her until 'this cruel war is over.' "[30]

It was aboard this ship that Belle met and fell in love with a young Federal officer, Lieutenant Samuel Hardinge. He helped her escape to Canada, and then make her way to England, where he later joined her. The couple married on August 25, 1864. Belle remained in England for two years where she wrote her memoirs of her adventures as a Civil War spy. Once the nation was reunited, Belle spent the rest of her life giving her countrymen this message of reconciliation: "One God, One Flag, One People—Forever."[31]

7

Emma Edmonds—Nurse and Spy

1861–1865	Civil War Union Army

President Lincoln had just declared war on the Southern states that had **seceded** from the Union. Thus began a bloody struggle between American countrymen, each side firmly believing it was right. The North was determined to keep the Union together. The South was determined to claim its Constitutional right to govern its own states. Slavery was a key issue, along with states' rights. Many battles were fought, many lives were lost, and many young men were wounded in the four-year struggle.

seceded: Separated

Emma Moves to the United States

Five years before the start of the Civil War, Sarah Emma Edmonds left her family's farm in New Brunswick, Canada, to move to the United States. She hoped to obtain a better education in the U.S. "An insatiable thirst for education led me to do this," she related in her memoirs.[32] For some reason, she chose to go by her second name, Emma. She took a job as a Bible salesman. Her boss claimed she was the best salesman he ever employed. Then something happened that changed her plans. Early in the spring of 1861, Emma heard that President Lincoln, having just declared war on the Confederacy, called for 75,000 men to volunteer as soldiers. At that news, she thought: "What can I do? What part am I to act in this great drama? I was not able to decide for myself—so I carried this question to the Throne of Grace and found a satisfactory answer there."[33]

The War Begins

Ten days after Lincoln issued his plea, Emma decided to **enlist** with the Michigan Volunteer Infantry as a field nurse. There was one problem, however. Only men were given this dangerous job. Emma, though just 21 years old, had never been afraid to take risks. So, she cut her hair short and disguised herself as a man. Taking the name of Franklin Thompson, she volunteered and requested an assignment to a field hospital. The recruiting sergeant, not spotting her disguise, informed her they desperately needed medical help. He told "Franklin" that he would enlist him as a field nurse. The following morning, she was headed for Washington by train with the other recruits to join the **Army of the Potomac**. Her unit consisted of the head surgeon Dr. Hodes, his assistant, four nurses, two cooks, a ward master, and an orderly who attended to heavy chores. The nurses worked in pairs for six-hour shifts around the clock.

enlist: Join up

Army of the Potomac: Main army of the Union

General George McClellan: General-in-chief of the Army of the Potomac

On to Fort Monroe

After several months, Emma's unit and many others were sent to Fort Monroe, located in Virginia between the York River and James River. **General George McClellan's** plan was to attack Richmond, the capital of the Confederacy. However, the city of Yorktown blocked his path.

A strong force led by **General Joseph Johnston** defended Yorktown. General McClellan was a very **cautious** man; he chose to continue to train and drill his troops rather than plan an attack.

In March 1860, Emma heard that a dear old friend with whom she had lost touch had come to her camp recently. She was very excited to see this cheerful person — he had always been a joy to be around. But at the same time, she was hoping he wouldn't recognize her disguise. Thoughts rushed through her mind: maybe he wouldn't . . . but if he did, she'd tell him her secret . . . she knew she could trust him.

General Joseph Johnston: Commander of the Army of Northern Virginia

cautious: Careful to avoid danger

She hurried to find him but instead found a group of soldiers standing around a fresh grave while the chaplain read a psalm. To her dismay, Emma found out that her friend, Lieutenant James Vesey, had been killed while out on patrol the previous night. Emma was stunned and saddened by the news. Tears began to flow as she stumbled back to camp.

Passing by the cabin of Chaplain Butler and his wife, Emma felt compelled to stop in. The chaplain often visited the wounded and was always so friendly to Emma. Noticing her distress, Mrs. Butler invited Emma to come in and offered her a cup of coffee, still thinking she was Franklin. Emma broke down in tears and told sympathetic Mrs. Butler her secret, and how crushed she was by James' death. A deep sense of relief flooded her now that someone else could share her secret. Mrs. Butler comforted her and assured her that the secret would be safe with her.

Becoming a Spy

Not long after, Chaplain Butler told 'Frank' that he heard of a job Frank might be interested in tackling. It was very dangerous and extremely important to the war effort. One of the Union's key spies had been captured in Richmond and shot. McClellan and the army were now without badly needed intelligence about the enemy. Someone had to fill the spy's place. Emma wrote, "I did consider it thoroughly, and made up my mind to accept it with all its fearful responsibilities. The subject of life and death was not weighed in the balance; I left that in the hands of my Creator, feeling assured that I was just as safe in passing the picket lines of the enemy, if it was God's will that

I should go there, as I would be in the Federal camp. And if not, then His will be done."[34] The next day Emma faced a panel of officers who asked her about her beliefs, patriotism, and feelings about the Union cause. They decided to give her a chance. She was given the freedom to choose her disguise and story. They told her to be ready in three days.

Disguised Again

Emma excitedly returned to Mrs. Butler, who helped her to plan her new disguise. She knew Confederate armies used slaves around the camps to do all sorts of labor. Best of all, officers felt free to talk around the slaves. So, Emma disposed of her 'Frank' disguise and with Mrs. Butler's help, became a slave named 'Cuff.' They acquired a curly black wig and suitable slave clothes. Emma got some silver nitrate from the hospital and applied it to make her skin dark. Mrs. Butler filled Emma's canvas sack with corncakes and dried apple slices. Giving Mrs. Butler a big hug, Emma hurried off to headquarters. An officer was given the task of guiding Emma, now Cuff, to the valley that led to the Confederate camp.

Behind Confederate Lines

'Cuff' managed to slip past the guards and joined some black men walking down the road. Emma was pretending to be Cuff and to be lost, and they welcomed 'Cuff' who seemed to fit right into their group. 'Cuff' labored along with the other slaves and was assigned the task of moving wheelbarrow loads of gravel all day long.

'Cuff' was very alert to any details in the camp that might be useful. The Confederates were building fortifications in preparation for fighting the Union army. It was hard work and by the end of the day, Emma's hands were raw and bleeding. All the workers were given one hour of freedom in the evening when work was done, and 'Cuff' made good use of it, wandering around camp and observing anything that might be useful to the Union. That night Emma carefully wrote down all she had observed: "twenty-five rifled three-inch cannons, eleven **Dahlgren guns**, twenty-nine 32-pounders, seven **siege howitzers**, fourteen heavy mortars, thirteen **columbiads**, many light weapons"[35] Then stuffing the notes she'd written under the lining of her shoes, she lay down to sleep.

Dahlgren guns: Muzzleloaders

siege howitzers: Heavy guns to bomb fortifications

columbiads: Muzzle loading cannons

The next day, 'Cuff' showed a worker in the kitchen blistered hands and begged him to swap jobs with him for the day. Feeling sorry for the young laborer, the worker agreed. That day was spent in taking meals to the crews who were manning heavy artillery. This gave 'Cuff' an opportunity to learn more about their fortifications as well as a chance to listen to conversations. Emma learned that General Robert E. Lee had visited Yorktown and didn't think Confederate defenses were strong enough yet. She also observed fake guns and made a point to remember where they were located. She recognized a peddler who was often in the Union camp and discovered that he was really a Confederate spy. She learned so much information that she now needed a plan to get back to Union lines undetected. Suddenly, a young Confederate lieutenant ran up, put a gun in 'Cuff's hands, and demanded 'Cuff' stand guard to fill a post where a sentry had just been shot. 'Cuff' was told to stand there until the officer could return with a replacement. God had provided the chance she needed! It was just getting dark when Emma hurried off across the field before the lieutenant had time to return.

Back to Union Lines

Back on the Union side, Emma told the sentry that she had important information for headquarters and was allowed to pass. Emma, now Frank again, pulled off a shoe and spread out all the hidden papers, to the colonel's delight. 'Frank' briefed the colonel about all the gun batteries, fortifications, number of soldiers, and locations of the fake guns. The general was informed that the trusted peddler was a Confederate spy! General McClelland personally came to shake 'Frank's' hand and offered to let 'Cuff' keep the gun which had been given by the sentry. Mrs. Butler was elated to learn that Emma was safe. She said she and Chaplain Butler had prayed often for 'Cuff's' safety.

Emma returned to nursing duty. Three days later, partly due to the intelligence Emma had gained, McClellan ordered an attack on the Confederates. The battle raged and casualties mounted. It took five weeks for the army of the Potomac to defeat Yorktown. McClellan's men then began their march to Richmond, the Confederate capital. When they were only three miles away, they realized they needed to know what type of defenses the Confederates had in Richmond. Someone would have to sneak into enemy lines to find out.

Another Dangerous Mission

It was May 20, 1862, when a rowboat, with pieces of a blanket tied to its oars to muffle sound, crossed quietly to the other side of the James River. There, a middle-aged woman climbed out, carrying a wicker basket. She walked along through the underbrush for a mile or so until she came to the road. Here she would rest until dawn.

Emma, **alias** Frank Thompson, alias Cuff, was now an Irish **peddler** named Bridget O'Shea. Mrs. Butler had tied a pillow around Emma's middle to make her appear plump, covering it

alias: False identity

peddler: Traveler selling merchandise

with a petticoat, fancy blouse, and long skirt. She wore a shawl over all that. Mrs. Butler had dusted flour in Emma's hair to make it appear grey. She finished the disguise with a pair of metal-rimmed glasses. In Bridget's basket were peddler's goods to sell to the Confederate soldiers — thread, needles, matches, scissors, soap, corncakes, and tea bags.

Her story was very believable because many Irish immigrants had recently come to America to escape the devastating potato famine that left many of their countrymen in poverty. When they arrived in this country, they did whatever work they could find to make a living.

Reaching the road, Bridget found what appeared to be a deserted house. It would be a safe place to rest. Inside, though, she found a young Confederate lieutenant dying from typhoid fever. She knew he was close to death and refused to leave him to die alone. She nursed him all that day and the next night until he passed. Before he died, he requested that she deliver a watch to Major McKee of **General Ewell's** staff. She told him she would try and headed for the Confederate camp. There she explained that she had to find Major McKee. An aide told her the major was out till later that afternoon and she should make herself at home at their camp.

General Ewell: Confederate general

Gladly, she made her way to where some women were cooking and washing. One of them brought her some food. Bridget carefully observed their clothing for possible future disguises. She learned from them the number of troops stationed there and the names of their officers. She wandered around selling her wares, watching, and listening, counting the cannons, noting the layout of defenses.

When Major McKee returned, Bridget gave him the watch and message. He was quite sad, but at least he now knew what had become of his friend, Lieutenant Allen Hall. Then he asked Bridget if she knew how to ride a horse. She did, of course, and he asked if she would be willing to guide his men to the house so they could bring the lieutenant's body to camp to bury him. Emma was thrilled, realizing this might just be a way for her to return to Union lines. As they rode, she asked the sergeant many questions. She learned the Confederates were hiding heavy guns in the woods to ambush the Yankees.

When they arrived at the house, the sergeant asked Emma to stand as a lookout while they loaded the body. He explained that the Yankees, if they happened along, would never shoot a woman. She consented, and they agreed she would catch up with them after the danger was gone. Marveling again at her opportunity, she waited until they were out of sight before racing the horse back to Union headquarters. Colonel Shrub, the **adjutant** received the information gratefully. He told her she could keep the fine chestnut horse, which she named 'Rebel.'

adjutant: Assistant to a general

As a spy, Emma went on nine more missions, each time wearing a different disguise and taking on a different assumed name. She "became" a Confederate soldier, a young Southern boy, a detective, a mail carrier, and a general's orderly. In 1863, she contracted a severe case of **malaria**. Fearing her secret would be discovered if she went to a camp hospital, she changed into women's clothes and checked herself into a civilian hospital. It took several weeks before she recovered. Emma planned to return to the army but learned that 'Frank Thompson' had been listed as a **deserter**. Deserters are usually imprisoned or punished severely. For the remainder of the war, Emma served as a nurse in Washington under her rightful name, caring for the wounded.

malaria: High fever caused by an infected mosquito bite

deserter: One who has left the army without permission

The War Ends

Emma rejoiced when the war ended, and the country was reunited. She began writing memoirs of her experiences as a spy. She dedicated her book to the sick and wounded soldiers she had served. She brought a manuscript to her old boss from her Bible-selling days, who gladly published it, selling 175,000 copies the first year. Emma donated all the proceeds to an organization that helped Civil War veterans. Emma married Linus Seelye, a carpenter, and an old childhood friend. They had three sons, one of whom joined the army, "just like Mama did."[36]

Emma became the first and only woman recognized as a veteran of the Civil War. She received a pension for her service. Emma was also the only woman invited to join the Grand Army of the Republic, an association for Civil War veterans of the Union army. Why did she risk so much? She tells us in her memoirs. "I am naturally fond of adventure, a little ambitious, and a good deal romantic — but patriotism was the true secret of my success."[37]

Dabney and Lucy Walker – Clothesline Spies

1863–1864	Fredericksburg, Virginia

Slaves Escape

In 1862, the Union army was stationed at Fredericksburg, Virginia, from April through August. During this time, more than 10,000 slaves escaped at a place called 'The Crossing.' The Crossing was a location along the Rappahannock River extending from Fredericksburg to Falmouth, Virginia. It was here that slaves from four counties — Spotsylvania, Caroline, Stafford, and Orange — would escape to freedom. Slaves used different forms of travel to get away. Some walked, some rode trains, and others rode horses. Still others were concealed in wagons at night under cover of darkness. Some wagon drivers who helped slaves escape covered them up with piles of hay. Others even had compartments built into the bottoms of their wagons which they would cover with produce to take to market.

The Underground Railroad

The Underground Railroad was a loose association of people established 30 years before the Civil War to help slaves run away to Canada or to free Northern states to attain freedom. It used many different routes through different states. Usually, it was organized and run by small groups of concerned citizens wanting to help. They used certain code words to describe their efforts. For instance, a 'pilot' was a person who went south seeking folks who wanted help to get to freedom. A 'conductor' was one who physically guided folks to freedom, navigating the roads and safe paths. The escaping people were called 'passengers,' and safe places used to hide them along the way were called 'stations.' This helped to keep the work secret, concealed from common knowledge. The process was very **stealthy**. Slaves learned about it by "word of mouth." It was in early 1863 that Dabney Walker, his wife, Lucy Ann, and their daughter Sarah managed to flee for their lives. They had been slaves on a farm in Spotsylvania County, Virginia. They crossed over into Union lines near Falmouth, Virginia.

stealthy: Secretive

Battle of Fredericksburg

The Battle of Fredericksburg was fought from December 11–15, 1862, under the Union command of Major General Ambrose Burnside. Burnside's plans went very wrong, and eventually wave after wave of Union soldiers attempting to take a main road were met with devastating artillery fire from Confederate soldiers who held a nearly **impregnable** position. As the day ended on December 14, Burnside, seeing the battlefield covered with dead Union soldiers, knew that he must **retreat** across the Rappahannock the next morning. This cnded the battle in a

impregnable: Not able to be attacked

retreat: Withdraw

Confederate victory. Six weeks later, President Lincoln replaced General Burnside with Major General Joseph Hooker, who took command of the Union Army of the Potomac.

It was under Major General Hooker's command that 52-year-old Dabney Walker, now a free man and a soldier in the Union army, was assigned to the camp's brand-new intelligence unit. Hooker realized that the army was greatly lacking in intelligence and didn't want a repeat of Fredericksburg. The Walkers were about to become one of Major General Joseph Hooker's most useful sources of information about the army of Northern Virginia.

Working for the Union Army

Dabney Walker was being trained in the value and use of signal flags to send coded messages to soldiers across the battlefield when he got an idea that proved to be invaluable. Dabney headed over to see his wife Lucy, who worked as a **laundress** for the camp. When they escaped into Union territory, Dabney started working first as a cook. Then he became a valued **scout**. Dabney had earned a

laundress: Woman who does laundry

scout: Person sent to gather information about the enemy reputation for being extremely **competent** at gaining intelligence, so much so that the Confederate army had recently offered a $1,500 reward (equivalent to over $59,000 today) to anyone able to capture him. Having grown up in Virginia, Dabney was indispensable because he knew the roads, and could find the hiding places of the Confederates. This was even more important now under the new general, who needed to know every movement and detail of General Robert E. Lee's army.

competent: Skillful

Dabney was excited and determined to be the best spy ever. Having escaped themselves, he and his wife Lucy were dedicated to helping end slavery for all their friends and relatives; therefore, they were willing to take risks to do it.

Becoming Spies

Dabney shared with Lucy what he had learned about how flags were used to deliver messages and his idea that there might be a way he and Lucy could communicate information using flags. Lucy was **intrigued** with the concept but thought there might be a better

intrigued: Fascinated

method for Dabney and herself to use. She had been a laundress for most of her life — why not use laundry as a signal? The idea was risky. Lucy would have to give up her freedom for a time. She would cross back into rebel territory and take on the job of laundress for the Confederate army. Then she could listen attentively and learn of troop movements and plans. The soldiers and officers never tried to hide plans from the slaves, not thinking them to be a threat. However, it was dangerous. Lucy and Dabney both knew if she were caught and found to be a spy, she would hang, but the **simplicity** of the plan and the reason for taking the risks outweighed her fear. Yes, they would have to take a risk, but they would be helping so many others to gain freedom. Yes, it just might work!

simplicity: Simple nature

The Clothesline Telegraph

The plan was beginning to take shape in their minds. They decided to use different colors of shirts to signal different things. For example, "gray for Confederate General James Longstreet; white for General A. P. Hill; and red for General "Stonewall Jackson."[38] They decided on a system to move each general's shirt to **signify** that he was moving his troops. When one was removed, that showed that he had moved his troops out of the area. If Lucy

signify: Indicate

moved one general's shirt further up the clothesline, that meant his troops had moved upstream. And so, it went. Another clothesline was devoted to General Lee, showing only his movements. His headquarters was just across the river from them. A single piece of laundry meant his troops were in the process of moving. Two pieces signified they weren't moving at all. Three would warn Dabney and thereby, the Union general, that Lee was adding numbers to the present troop count. Finally, they were satisfied with their signals and ready to put the plan into action.

Now came the tricky part. Somehow, they would have to get Lucy back across the river to join the Confederate army. A safe opportunity soon came. The Union soldiers were helping a Southern woman who was living in Union-occupied territory to travel across the river to visit her friends. Lucy posed as her servant as they helped the woman on the boat that would take her across the river. For some reason, no one questioned Lucy. When she arrived in the camp, she just joined in with the other women, acting as if she'd been there all along. Soon Lucy was doing laundry and cooking for General Lee and his men.

Ready to Spy

The plan worked perfectly. The Union officers were amazed at how quickly Dabney began providing information about Confederate troop movements and plans. They began to wonder how he was getting such accurate information so quickly. "Within an hour of the time that a movement of any kind was projected, or even discussed among the rebel generals, Hooker knew all about it. He knew which corps were moving, or about to move in, in what direction, how long they had been on the march, and in what force; and all this knowledge came through Dabney, and all his reports turned out to be true."[39]

For quite a while Dabney wouldn't tell anyone how he was doing it. He wanted to keep Lucy as safe as possible and the fewer people who knew, the better the chance he had of doing that. Finally, one day he took one of the officers with him as he climbed to a high hill, took his binoculars, and gazed across the river at a clothesline. He pointed out a little cabin in the suburbs near the riverbank and asked him if he saw that clothesline with clothes hanging on it. "That clothesline tells me in half an hour just what goes on at Lee's headquarters. You see, my wife over there; she washes for the officers, and cooks, and waits around, and as soon as she hears about any movement or anything going on, she comes down and moves the clothes on the line so I can understand it in a minute. That there gray shirt is Longstreet; and when she takes it off, it means he's gone down about Richmond. That white shirt means Hill; and when she moves it up to the west end of the line, Hill's corps has moved up the stream. That red one is Stonewall. He's on the right now, and if he moves, she will move that red shirt."[40]

Lucy heard much information by listening closely. The servants of officers also would willingly share bits of information they heard while tending to officers to whom they were assigned. Carefully, so as not to attract attention, Lucy would head off to her clothesline. She always kept clothes on the line so as not to raise suspicion.

Dabney and Lucy had even worked out a coded way to communicate that the Confederates were doing things to confuse the Union, like pretending to move, just to mislead the enemy. As one of Union officers related, "One morning Dabney came in and reported a movement over there. But it don't amount to anything. They're just making believe. Do you see those blankets pinned together at the bottom? That's her way of making a fish-trap; and when she pins the clothes together in this way, it means that Lee is only trying to draw us into his fish-trap."[41]

Where Is the Laundry?

The system was working wonderfully well. One day, however, the laundry wasn't there. Dabney was so worried that Lucy had been discovered — maybe even hanged. He prayed often. Then several days later the laundry appeared again! Dabney was overjoyed. His precious wife was still alive and well. It was never recorded why the laundry had stopped for those days, so that remains a mystery. In the spring of 1863, Hooker prepared to lead his troops into battle, feeling well-supplied with information from the Walkers and his other spies.

In June, the Union army left Virginia. Dabney and Lucy's services were no longer needed. An officer praised the couple for being among the "promptest and most reliable" of General Hooker's spies.[42] Lucy somehow managed to escape back to the Union lines, and she and Dabney headed to their home in Washington, D.C. Lucy continued to work as a laundress and Dabney as a carpenter. Dabney was again needed as a scout when the Union army tried to take over Richmond, Virginia, in May 1864. No one knows if Lucy went with him or stayed at home for this campaign.

Dabney was **instrumental** in starting Fifth Avenue Baptist Church (now known as Vermont Avenue Baptist) in Washington, D.C., along with some other formerly enslaved men. Their daughter Sarah was married there in 1871. Lucy Ann died on June 12, 1880, at age 66. Dabney lived to be 74 and died on April 23, 1885. They are buried, along with their daughter and grandchildren, at Mt. Plains Cemetery, Walter Pierce Park, in Washington, D.C.

instrumental: Involved in

World War II

World War II was a global conflict that occurred from 1939 to 1945. It involved many countries around the world. The main countries that created the conflict were called the Axis powers, led by Germany, Italy, and Japan. The other countries, like the United States, United Kingdom, and the Soviet Union, were called the Allies and rose up to try to stop the Axis nations.

The war started when Germany invaded Poland, and soon other countries got involved. There were battles in Europe, Africa, and Asia. A deeply tragic part of the war was the Holocaust, where the Nazis, who were in charge of Germany, began to kill many people, including millions of Jews, Romani people, and disabled people.

The United States joined the war after the attack on Pearl Harbor in 1941. It was a difficult time in history, and many people worked together to stop the powerful Axis nations. There were big battles like D-Day, where the Allies landed in France to push back the Germans.

In 1945, the war finally ended. The Allies won, and the world worked together to make sure something like this wouldn't happen again. World War II changed the world, and it's important to remember the people who fought and died for our peace today.

9

The Ghost Army

1944	From Normandy to the Rhine River, France

The world was **embroiled** in World War II. Hitler, the German dictator, was determined to overpower European nations and become their leader. He was well-organized and motivated to do just that. Something had to be done to stop him. The Allied nations joined together and **brainstormed** ideas that might give them a victory. There had to be a way to outsmart the Germans before all the European nations lost their freedom and fell into his hands.

embroiled: Deeply involved

brainstormed: Shared thoughts

A Different Kind of Spy Work

Spy work takes many different forms, often extremely creative. The **D-Day Invasion** had just begun. A huge wave of Allied soldiers had crossed the English Channel to invade the coast of France in a massive effort to take France back from **Nazi** control. It included a highly organized array

D-Day Invasion: Largest Allied land, air, and sea invasion in military history

Nazi: Member of German Worker's Party

of planes, boats, **gliders**, and parachutists to land soldiers on Omaha Beach.

At first, it proved disastrous. There were many **casualties**. Hundreds of men lost their lives as they landed on the beaches of Normandy, and many others were wounded. The men of the 603rd Engineer Camouflage Battalion witnessed the devastation as they arrived on the beach about a week after the first wave of men had landed. The men from the 603rd platoon had trained for weeks for the mission they were here to fulfill. Theirs was a fairly new and unproven type of warfare.

They had been ordered to fight the war with guns, tanks, and planes made of inflatable rubber! Yes, rubber — they looked like blow-up toys, not weapons of war. There were about 1,000 men assigned to this secret deception unit, code-named 'Blarney.' They came to test their idea, to see if they could fool the Germans into thinking inflatable weapons were the real thing. They began setting up their fake guns a mile ahead of the army's actual line to trick the Germans into firing on them instead of the real artillery unit behind them!

gliders: Engineless aircraft to transport men

casualties: Injuries

Top-Secret Project

The men who had dreamed up this mission were the 23rd Headquarters Special Troops, nicknamed 'The Ghost Army.' 'Ghost' referred to the fact that they appeared to be a fighting unit, they appeared to have many men

and weapons, but it was all fake. No one knew if the idea would work.

The men had trained in England, but they hadn't been trained as soldiers. This was a unique group of carefully selected and highly intelligent men chosen for their skills in art, painting, and design. For two whole years, this unit developed its skills in creating and testing inflatable guns, tanks, planes, and vehicles. Some of the team had practiced camouflaging military sites in the United States in preparation for their task. Using their artistic skills, they were able to disguise bomber planes and military bases to the point that spy planes couldn't see them from the air.

More Units Added

Other units were employed to help with the project — the signal company and the **sonic** company. The signal company consisted of highly skilled radio operators whose job was to imitate the radio **transmissions** of whatever unit the Ghost Army was called upon to impersonate. The Germans

sonic: Having to do with sound

transmissions: Messages

were skillful at listening to Allied radio transmissions to gain intelligence. Now, the hope was that the Germans who were spying on Allied communications would believe there was a unit in the location where the Ghost Army had set up camp. The real unit, meanwhile, would be free to relocate to a better position without being detected.

The Germans were very skilled at observing how different units sent transmissions. They could recognize the nicknames for men in various units and could even identify the way an operator tapped out **Morse code**. The Ghost Army operators had to duplicate the real unit's habits exactly to avoid suspicion. Getting all the details right meant not only safeguarding their own lives, but the lives of many soldiers in other units.

Morse code: Code for letters

The sonic company was responsible for sound effects. They had spent months recording different sounds: units of men moving into camp, bridges being built, orders being given, tanks moving around, trucks starting up, and even officers shouting orders. Their job was to convince the enemy to believe that a large force was there when it really wasn't. They played the sounds from speakers mounted on specially created trucks called half-tracks that had wheels on the front and tracks like those of a tank on the back. Weathermen were part of this unit because wind and temperature greatly affected how well sound traveled. Much attention was given to even the smallest detail.

Another unit in this Ghost Army was the combat company. There were about 200 men who provided security, the only men in the Ghost Army actually trained to fight as soldiers. They kept curious civilians from wandering into the camp to see inflatable tanks. They also dug real tank and artillery positions for the fake equipment. Explosions were set off so it would appear that the 'rubber' guns were firing. It was quite a **sophisticated** set-up — and dangerous. Their mission was to get the Germans to fire at them although they didn't have the means or expertise to fire back. When all was ready, the men held their breath to see if the Germans would be fooled and begin firing at them. The first shell landed, then another, then another — it was working! That month the unit fooled the Germans at ten different sites as they traveled up the French peninsula. All the men of the Ghost Army survived that first operation with no casualties, and without firing a single gun!

sophisticated: Complex

Refining their Efforts

The men soon realized that they hadn't considered the fact that inflatable tanks don't make tracks in the dirt, so they began using their bulldozers to make tracks for the fake tanks. Another man pointed out that if guns were firing, surely shell casings would be scattered all over the ground, so the Ghost Army began spreading used artillery shells all around their fake guns. Soldiers in the camps built many fires to lead the Germans to assume that many soldiers were camped there.

Soldiers also needed clean clothes. Clotheslines were strung and laundry was hung up. Real tanks would never sit out without being camouflaged, so the men began covering the inflatable tanks with camouflage netting. At one point, they were doing such skillful work at camouflaging that Allied planes couldn't spot any equipment, so they had to find a balance between using camouflage, while still allowing their equipment to be seen by the German spy planes. Charts were made for each unit they were called upon to impersonate so the soldiers would know how to imitate them. Information included markings on their vehicles, how their signs were painted, how they wore their uniforms, and how they talked to one another.

The Allies Break Through

Seven weeks after the D-Day landings, the Allies broke through the German lines. **General George Patton's** army now needed to march through France to surround German troops and defeat them. The element of surprise was needed and that's where the Ghost Army came in. Its next job was to make the Germans think the Allies planned to head west, not east. If they succeeded, then the German army would send men to the west and therefore have fewer men

General George Patton: Commander of the U.S. army after the Normandy invasion

available when Patton struck from the east.

The Ghost Army began its job of trickery. The signal men stayed busy sending fake radio messages, hoping the Germans would be listening in. More than 70 tanks were inflated. Bumpers of trucks and jeeps were **stenciled** with the markings of the division they were impersonating.

stenciled: Decorated

Members of the Ghost Army freely wandered the streets of the town wearing patches on their shirts bearing the division's insignia of the unit they were pretending to belong to. If not, enough patches were available, the painters in the unit set to work painting patches on shirts and coats.

When the Germans began to fire, the Ghost Army knew it was succeeding in fooling the enemy. The Ghost Army kept the Germans right where they wanted them long enough for Patton to surround them. When the Germans realized they were surrounded, it was too late to wait for reinforcements to arrive. They were forced to retreat, and in their hurry to get away, they left behind all sorts of equipment. 50,000 Germans were captured; the rest were retreating to safety. The Allies were sweeping across France, and with them went the Ghost Army, bringing freedom to the French people.

More Campaigns

Toward the end of August, the Ghost Army impersonated an **armored** division to fool a German general into thinking he was facing many more tanks than the Americans actually had. The Ghost Army traveled through driving rain to their intended campsite. Upon arrival, the sonic team began playing the sound of a whole convoy of tanks arriving, bushes crackling, gears shifting, bridges being constructed, and officers hollering orders.

armored: Tank

The men stayed up all night long employing their special effects which would lead the enemy to believe a large army was present. The special effects consisted of fires, as groups of men would have to stay warm. It also included hanging up laundry to dry as large groups of men would need clean dry clothes. Tents were another special effect. Large groups of men had to sleep somewhere and of course they would have many tents set up for sleeping and protection from the cold. Suddenly the Germans began firing upon the fake camp and relocating their anti-tank guns to shoot at the Ghost Army, away from the site of the real fighting. While the Ghost Army held its position outside the French port city of Brest, the Allies were successful in liberating Paris! Paris was free and its citizens were joyfully celebrating.

Filling the Gap

The war wasn't over yet though. Patton was still on the move across France, and he was advancing so quickly that parts of the army couldn't keep up. A hole had developed in his defenses, north of the city of Metz. If the Germans found that gap, they could surround

Patton and defeat the Allies. If that happened there was no telling how much longer the war would drag on or how many more lives might be lost. The Ghost Army was needed again. The fate of Patton's army was at stake.

The Ghost Army had never impersonated an entire division before, but fortunately, it would only be a couple of days before a real unit would arrive to relieve them. They knew they would be on the front lines under **scrutiny** of the Germans. If they were detected now, it could **compromise** the rest of the war effort, not to mention their own lives. They had to travel 250 miles from their camp outside of Paris to Bettembourg, Luxembourg, to join the front line. The Germans were dangerously close, only about two miles away, but the Ghost Army knew lives were depending on the success of this mission. They began working furiously during the wee hours of the morning. The sonic crew began broadcasting the sounds of vehicles crashing through the forest and officers yelling out orders. It all sounded so real!

scrutiny: Watchful eyes

compromise: Endanger

Some of the men were frantically sewing patches on shirts, spreading spent shells, and flinging camouflage nets to cover inflatable equipment. All that day, the Ghost Army did everything possible to put up a good front. Fires were lit, laundry hung, signs posted, military checkpoints set up, and water stations created. They even painted markings of the Sixth Armored Division on their trucks. The men began socializing in restaurants in town and talking with civilians, bragging about their unit, and telling folks how massive troop reinforcements were moving in that night. The Germans were camped just across the river, listening, and watching. That night, the sound effects led the Germans to believe that many trucks, tanks, and men were arriving. The next day was Sunday. The Germans began moving in more troops to be ready for an attack.

The Ghost Army only had to hang on one more day when the real division was due to arrive. Unfortunately, they were delayed! The Ghost Army fearfully scrambled to keep up the sound effects and appearances, trying to hang on, but they could see that the Germans were getting restless, and the situation was growing more and more **perilous**. Finally, after seven long days, the 83rd Infantry arrived. The Ghost Army, armed with only radios, paint, and creativity, had succeeded in keeping the Germans at bay!

perilous: desperately dangerous

Crossing the Rhine

The Ghost Army faithfully fulfilled more missions in France. The final assault of the Allies against German forces was crossing the Rhine River. One by one, Allied soldiers crossed the Rhine into Germany, expecting to encounter heavy resistance. Instead, the Germans seemed surprised, as if they had expected the attack to come from elsewhere. That final crossing into Germany was accomplished with very little loss of life, and the war was soon over. From examining German documents after the war, the Allies found out why the Germans were unprepared. The Germans thought the bulk of the Ninth army was ten miles south of the actual crossing location — exactly where the Ghost Army had carried out their last mission.

The Ghost Army took part in 22 large-scale deceptions in Europe from Normandy to the Rhine River. It was instrumental in freeing Europe from the tyranny of Nazi invasion. "Following the war, the unit's soldiers were sworn to secrecy, records were classified, and equipment packed away. Except for a newspaper article right after the war, no one spoke publicly about the Ghost Army until a 1985 *Smithsonian* article. Though knowledge of the 23rd Headquarters Special Troops was then public, it was still officially classified until the mid-1990s."[43] Their story, hidden from the public, disappeared into our country's "Top Secret" files as though they had never existed for the next 50 years—a fitting end of the amazing Ghost Army. The National World War II Museum located in New Orleans, Louisiana, has an exhibit dedicated to the memory of the Ghost Army and their contribution to Allied victory, as does the National Spy Museum in Washington D.C.

On Tuesday, February 1, 2022, President Biden signed into law bill S. 1404, the "Ghost Army Congressional Gold Medal Act," which provides for the award of a Congressional Gold Medal to the "Ghost Army," in recognition of their unique and highly distinguished service in conducting deception operations in Europe during World War II.

10

The Navajo Code Talkers

1944–1945	From Guadalcanal to Iwo Jima

World War II

The United States had joined the **Allies** during World War II, after Japanese planes attacked their naval base at Pearl Harbor, Hawaii, on December 7, 1941. More than 2,000 American soldiers and sailors were killed. Many battles were fought on the Pacific islands, as they were the ideal sites for the Japanese to launch attacks against American ships and planes. The Americans wanted to build military bases on these islands to make it easier to fight closer to Japan. Some of the hardest-fought battles of the war took place there. As always with war, intelligence was a key factor in determining which side would win. The Navajo Code Talkers made the difference for the United States and played a part in every major battle fought in the Pacific.

Allies: Great Britain, United States, Soviet Union

The Navajo Nation

The "Navajo Nation" is land restored to the Navajo Indians by the United States in a treaty signed in 1868, assuring that they would be free to live and keep their traditions, language, and faith. It includes parts of Utah, Colorado, Arizona, and New Mexico. When World War II began, the Navajo men were ready to join the fight. They made this official statement: "We resolve that the Navajo

Indians stand ready as they did in 1918, to aid and defend our government and Constitution against all...armed conflict."[44]

Philip Johnston, whose father was a missionary to the Navajo people, had grown up in the Navajo Nation. He was a veteran of World War I and remembered hearing of the success of the Choctaw Code Talkers who had developed code in their language. So, he suggested to the Marine commanders that they employ Navajo soldiers to use their native language to develop an unbreakable code.

Before World War II the Navajo language had never been written down. The people memorized information to pass on to their children and had become highly skilled in remembering and communicating orally by telling stories. This was a great benefit to those who developed the code. Only 30 people who were not Navajo by birth could even speak the language. One of the code talkers, Chester Nez, explained, "The language was not written, it could not be learned from a book... [Saying] even one Navajo word is nearly impossible for someone not used to hearing the sounds that make up the language."[45]

Johnston arranged a demonstration to try to convince Marine Corps officers to consider his idea. Four Navajo speakers were able to translate a test message from English into Navajo in 20 seconds. Non-Navajo code workers, using a code already in use, took half an hour to translate the same message. Twenty seconds was enough to impress the commanding officers. Twenty-nine Navajo men were selected for a top-secret, dangerous mission. These were the men who would develop a secret code that proved to be impossible for the enemy to understand.

Training

At first, training was very hard on the Navajo men. Navajo people hardly ever raise their voices. The new soldiers had to get used to being yelled at by their drill instructors. They also weren't used to having every minute of their day planned out for them. The hard work wasn't challenging for them, though, and they enjoyed the food they were given. They proved to be well-skilled as **marksmen**. They had grown up hunting. Their platoon scored high marks in pistol and rifle shooting. They also were excellent at **improvising** during desert training. When the other Marines came back with empty **canteens**, the Navajo men had filled their canteens with water they **extracted** from cactus plants. Marching and running long distances were easy for the Navajos as well. After ten weeks of training at Camp Pendleton, in North San Diego County in Southern California, one of the men's training commanders told them, "Yours has been one of the most outstanding platoons in the history of this Recruit Depot. . . . You obey orders like seasoned and disciplined soldiers. You have maintained rugged health. . .. The Marine Corps is proud to have you in our ranks."[46]

A few days later the men were transferred to Camp Elliott in San Diego, California, where they were **briefed** on their secret mission. Most of the codes the United States had used up until this time had been broken already by the Japanese. When the enemy learns the plans of the other side, many lives can be lost.

marksmen: People skilled in shooting guns

improvising: Using what's available

canteens: Personal water containers

extracted: Drew from

briefed: Informed of details

The Navajo Marines were told their job was to create an unbreakable code using their Navajo words — a code the Japanese could not break. They spent months creating this complex code.

Each letter of the English alphabet was given an English code word starting with that letter, making use of the names of common words — animals, plants, objects. The English code words were then translated into Navajo. For the letter 'A' they used the Navajo word for ant, 'wol-la-chee.' 'B' became bear or 'shush' in the Navajo language. They "also invented code words for common military objects. The Navajo word for hummingbird was chosen for fighter plane. A battleship was a whale, a hand grenade was a potato, and a bomb was an egg."[47] They came up with more than 200 code words for words commonly used in the army such as hospital, river, and troops.

As one of the men explained, "In Navajo, everything is in the memory — songs, prayers, everything. That's the way we were raised."[48] Much of the Navajo culture had been based on oral storytelling. Even lists of things to remember were never written down. After creating the code, the men spent hours memorizing hundreds of these words so they would know them instantly on the battlefield. Sometimes they worked 35-hour shifts without rest, but they knew thousands of lives were depending on their accuracy.

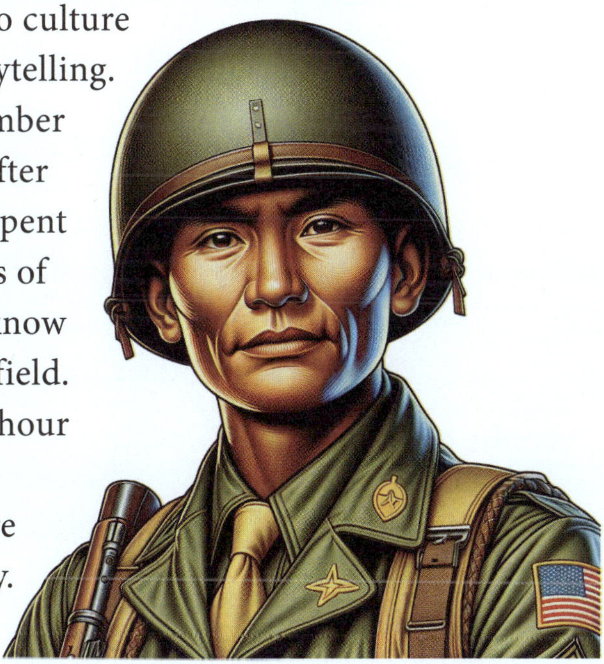

On to the Pacific

In October 1942, code talkers, 27 in all, were sent on to the Pacific while others stayed behind to train more **recruits**. After a long sea voyage, many suffering from seasickness, they arrived in November at Guadalcanal, part of the Solomon Islands, to implement their first mission. The U.S. military had recently landed there, but much of the island was still held by the Japanese.

The code talkers worked around the clock in teams of two setting up communication posts with two-way radios. Soldiers would carry the 35-pound radios in large backpacks. Chester Nez recalled his first coded transmission. "Enemy machine-gun nests on your right flank. Destroy. (In Navajo, "Beh-na-ali-tsosie-a-knah-as-donih ah-toh nish-na-jih-goh dah-di-kad ah-deel-tahi")"[49] Another team received his message and relayed it to the artillery unit, and the machine gun nest was destroyed within minutes!

recruits: New soldiers

platoon: Unit of soldiers

The next two days were almost sleepless, as they sent message after message: send more ammunition, aim here, move this **platoon** to another area, etc. With their careful messages, they directed artillery fire and helped to position troops, saving countless lives. With the help of the code talkers, U.S. Marines defeated the Japanese on Guadalcanal in February 1943. After securing Guadalcanal, Marine Major General Alexander Vandegrift sent this message back to Camp Elliot: "This Navajo code is terrific. The enemy never understood it. We don't understand it either, but it works. Send us some more Navajos."[50]

On to Iwo Jima

The Japanese were doing everything they could to stop the code talkers from doing their job. They heard all the communications the Navajos were sending, but they couldn't understand a word of it. So, in order to try to disrupt the code talkers' concentration, the Japanese banged pots and pans to make loud noises on their radio broadcasts. The code talkers began to worry about what would happen if they were caught. The Japanese might try to force them to reveal the code by hurting them. Because this was a real possibility and realizing how **vital** the code talkers had become to the

vital: Necessary

war effort, Marine bodyguards were assigned to them to protect them from enemy attack. The army commanders realized just how valuable these soldiers were when they ordered the extra layer of protection to ensure Allied victory.

The Marines' next target in their **island-hopping strategy** was Iwo Jima. It is a tiny island that lies 760 miles from Japan's capital city Tokyo. It was created by an exploding volcano and means "sulfur island" in Japanese. The Americans desperately wanted to secure this island so they could send out bomber planes in easy reach of Japan. They felt that the war might end sooner if they could capture this island but knew it would not be easy. 20,000 Japanese soldiers were occupying the tiny island. U.S. airplanes began bombing it, but the Japanese had dug thousands of tunnels and caves to hide in and they were fierce soldiers trained to fight to the death.

island-hopping strategy: Plan to take the islands one at a time

Navajo code talkers were among the first Marines to land on Iwo Jima.

During the first two days of the

invasion, the code talkers worked for 24 hours without sleeping. The fighting was intense with many casualties. The code talkers had to dig **foxholes** before they could begin relaying messages. The messages they transmitted were specific to what was taking place. They included calling for help for wounded men and directing ships and planes as to where to send their bombs. With bullets flying all about them, they sent messages between different troops on different parts of the island. "Need bulldozer on Green Beach immediately."

foxholes: Holes in the ground for protection

Marine commanders got the message and sent a bulldozer to Green Beach where it knocked down barriers the enemy had built. "Receiving steady machine gun and rifle fire." A group of Marines were sent to the machine gun nest to attack it, stopping the enemy fire, and saving dozens of U.S. soldiers. The code talkers sent and decoded over 800 messages without making any mistakes in the first two days of the mission. Finally, on the fifth day, Marines cheered as they raised a flag on Mount Suribachi, the highest point on the island. After it was over, Major Howard Conner declared, "Were it not for the Navajos, the Marines would never have taken Iwo Jima."[51]

The War Ends

World War II ended when the Japanese surrendered on August 14, 1945. Over 11,000 American soldiers had given their lives. Thirteen Navajo code talkers were among the dead. Many of the code talkers received medals for acts of heroism. When they were sent home, however, they were told they must keep their service a secret, not even telling family members how they had served. The military needed to keep the code a secret in case it was needed at a future time. They did keep their story secret for more than 20 years. In 1968, the government allowed the story of the code talkers to be told.

In 1971, 69 of the code talkers formed the *Navajo Code Talkers Association*. Its mission was to inspire young Navajo men and all Americans to be brave. They visited schools, marched in parades, and were interviewed on radio and TV. President Ronald Reagan set aside August 14 to be National Navajo Code Talkers Day and encouraged the people of the United States to honor this special group of war heroes. In 2001, the original 29 were awarded the **Congressional Medal of Honor**. All of the others received silver medals. On the back of the medals were the words, "With the Navajo language they defeated the enemy."[52] It was time for the country to give honor to whom honor was due. Their story still serves to inspire a grateful America today.

Congressional Medal of Honor: given for outstanding bravery in combat

Glossary

adjutant: Assistant to a general

alias: False identity

Allies: Great Britain, United States, Soviet Union

armored: Tank

Army of the Potomac: Main army of the Union

barracks: Living quarters

barricades: Objects lined up to prevent troops from getting past them

birds-eye view: View from above

blockaded: Sealed off

bottled up: Trapped

brainstormed: Shared thoughts

briefed: Informed of details

canteens: Personal water containers

casualties: Injuries

cautious: Careful to avoid danger

cavalry: Soldiers on horseback

cipher: Where each letter in a message is replaced by another letter or number

civilian: Non-military

colonies: Areas under the full or partial political control of another country

columbiads: Muzzle loading cannons

Commissary of Prisoners: Office established to handle prisoners and find intelligence

competent: Skillful

compromise: Endanger

comrade: Fellow soldier

conceal: Hide

confiscating: Secretly taking

Congressional Medal of Honor: Given for outstanding bravery in combat

Continentals: Patriot colonists

converted: Changed

conveying: Gathering and reporting

count: Military commander

courier: Messenger

crossfire: Gunfire from two directions

Dahlgren guns: Muzzleloaders

D-Day Invasion: Largest Allied land, air, and sea invasion in military history

decipher: Decode

delegate: Elected official sent to represent others

deserter: One who has left the army without permission

designs: Plans

detained: Forced to stay

disguise: To alter one's dress or appearance to conceal one's true identity

disinformation: Inaccurate data

dispatches: Important written messages

drawing room: Large room for entertaining

eavesdrop: Listen secretly

elite: Superior in training and abilities

embroiled: Deeply involved

enlist: Join up

escort: Guide for protection

extinguish: Put out

extracted: Drew from

ferrous sulfate: Green iron salt

fervor: Great loyalty

fictitious: Pretended

fortifying: Strengthening

foxholes: Holes in the ground for protection

French and Indian War: War between French, Indians, and British for territory in the Ohio Valley

General Ewell: Confederate general

General George McClellan: General-in-chief of the army of the Potomac

General George Patton: Commander of the U.S. army after the Normandy invasion

General Joseph Johnston: Commander of the army of Northern Virginia

gliders: Engineless aircraft to transport men

hushed: Quiet

implementation: Putting into use

implicate: Expose

impregnable: Not able to be attacked

improvising: Using what's available
incessant: Non-stop
ingenious: Clever
instrumental: Involved in
intel: Information
intelligence: Information about the enemy
intrigued: Fascinated
island-hopping strategy: Plan to take the islands one at a time
laundress: Woman who does laundry
light brigade: Officers who traveled light and fast
malaria: High fever caused by an infected mosquito bite
manors: Large country house with lands
marksmen: People skilled in shooting guns
midwife: Delivers babies
militia: Groups of men who protected their communities
monitor: Keep an eye on
morale: General mood among soldiers
Morse code: Code for letters
Nazi: Member of German Worker's Party
needle book: Fabric book for keeping sewing needles
oppressive: Unjust hardship
paroled: Released from duty
Patriots: Supporters of the colonies' rights
patronized: Frequently visited for business
peddler: Traveler selling merchandise
pensions: Retirement money

pensions: Retirement money

perilous: Desperately dangerous

petticoat: Garment worn under a dress for extra warmth

pillaging: Stealing

platoon: Unit of soldiers

Provost-Marshal: Union army officer in charge of maintaining order for soldiers and citizens

pursued: Chased

quartered: British soldiers living in colonists' homes without colonists' consent

reconciliation: Peace

recruited: Asked to join

recruits: New soldiers

Redcoats: British soldiers so called because of their red military jackets

redoubts: Temporary fortifications

regiment: Large group of soldiers divided into various units

retreat: Withdraw

ridge: Top

Royal Rangers: Loyalist military unit of the American Revolutionary War

rural: Country rather than city

safeguards: Measures taken to protect someone

scantily: Simply

scout: Person sent to gather information about the enemy

scrutiny: Watchful eyes

seceded: Separated

Second Continental Congress: Colonial delegates that formally met to decide issues of independence

Second Dragoons: Elite force of troops on horseback

sentries: Guards

shorthand: Method of rapid writing by using abbreviations and symbols

siege howitzers: Heavy guns to bomb fortifications

signify: Indicate

simplicity: Simple nature

sloop: Small sailing warship

sonic: Having to do with sound

sophisticated: Complex

spy: Person who secretly reports information on activities, movements, and plans of an enemy

spymaster: Head of an organization of spies

stealthy: Secretive

stenciled: Decorated

The Stonewall Brigade: Famous combat unit led by General Thomas 'Stonewall' Jackson.

strategic: Carefully designed to achieve military advantage

suspicion: Distrust

sympathies: Feelings

target: Person selected as the aim of an attack

Tory: American colonist who supported the British side during the American Revolution

traitorous: Disloyal

transmissions: Messages

Village Green: Area in center of town used for community events

vital: Necessary

Wallabout Bay: Small body of water- later known as the Brooklyn Navy Yard

Yankees: Confederate word for Union soldiers

Corresponding Curriculum

The *What a Character! Series* can be used alongside other Master Books curriculum for reading practice or to dive deeper into topics that are of special interest to students.

This book in the series features American war heroes, whose stories would incorporate well for students in grades 6-8 accompanying history, language arts, vocabulary words and definitions, as well as geography studies and cultural insights. We have provided this list below to help match this book with related Master Books curriculum.

Chapter 1: Nathan Hale— Spy and Hero

America's Story Vol. 1
The World's Story
The Fight for Freedom
World Geography and Cultures
Language Lessons for a Living Education
America's Struggle to Become a Nation

Chapter 2: Lydia Darragh — Quaker Spy

America's Story Vol. 1
The World's Story
The Fight for Freedom
World Geography and Cultures
Language Lessons for a Living Education
America's Struggle to Become a Nation

Chapter 3: Washington's Spies — The Culper Ring

America's Story Vol. 1
The World's Story
The Fight for Freedom
World Geography and Cultures
Language Lessons for a Living Education
America's Struggle to Become a Nation

Chapter 4: Anna Strong — Petticoat Spy

America's Story Vol. 1
The World's Story
The Fight for Freedom
World Geography and Cultures
Language Lessons for a Living Education
America's Struggle to Become a Nation

Chapter 5: James Armistead Lafayette—Double Spy

America's Story Vol. 1
The World's Story
The Fight for Freedom
World Geography and Cultures
Language Lessons for a Living Education
America's Struggle to Become a Nation

Chapter 6: Belle Boyd — Teen-aged Spy

America's Story Vol. 2
The World's Story
World Geography and Cultures
Language Lessons for a Living Education

Chapter 7: Emma Edmonds—Nurse and Spy

America's Story Vol. 2
The World's Story
World Geography and Cultures
Language Lessons for a Living Education

Chapter 8: Dabney and Lucy Walker — Clothesline Spies

America's Story Vol. 2
The World's Story
World Geography and Cultures
Language Lessons for a Living Education

Chapter 9: The Ghost Army

America's Story Vol. 3
The World's Story
World Geography and Cultures
Language Lessons for a Living Education

Chapter 10: The Navajo Code Talkers

America's Story Vol. 3
The World's Story
Language Lessons for a Living Education
Elementary U.S. Geography and Social Studies

Endnotes

1. Blaisdell and Ball, *Hero Stories from American History* (Boston: Ginn and Co., 1903) p. 55.
2. Shannon Zemlicka, *Nathan Hale: Patriot Spy* (Minneapolis, Minnesota: Millbrook Press, 2002) p. 34.
3. William Mace, *Mace's Beginners History* (New York: Rand McNally, 1909) p. 182.
4. Henry Darrach, *Lydia Darragh: One of the Heroines of the Revolution* (Philadelphia: Society of Friends, 1916) p. 391.
5. Ibid. 391.
6. Edith Patterson Meyer, *Petticoat Patriots of the American Revolution* (New York: The Vanguard Press, 1976) p. 90.
7. Darrach, *Lydia Darragh: One of the Heroines of the Revolution*, p. 393-394.
8. Thomas B. Allen, *George Washington, Spymaster*, (Washington D.C., National Geographic 2004) p. 16-17.
9. Ibid. p. 31-32.
10. Ibid. p. 69-70.
11. Brian Kilmeade and Don Yaeger, George *Washington's Secret Six: The Spies Who Saved America* adapted for Young Readers (New York: Viking, Random House 2019) p. 130-131.
12. Ibid. intro to book.
13. Frederic Gregory Mather, *The Refugees of 1776 from Long Island to Connecticut* (Albany, NY: J.B. Lyon Company, 1913), p. 582. A report by Mr. Selah B. Strong, grandson of Selah and Anna.
14. Beverly Tyler, A Case for Anna Smith Strong (Three Village Historical Society Articles, https://www.tvhs.org/archives)
15. James R. Gaines, *Liberty and Glory: Washington, Lafayette, and Their Revolutions* (New York: W. W. Norton & Company, 2007) p. 37.
16. Scarlet Ingstad, *The Indispensable Spy: The Story of James Armistead* (Monee, IL: Novella—independently published, 2021) p. 14.
17. https://www.mountvernon.org/library/digitalhistory/digital-encyclopedia/article/battle-of-the-chesapeake/
18. Burke Davis, *Black Heroes of the American Revolution* (New York: Harcourt, 1976) p. 53.
19. Ibid. p. 54.
20. Ibid. p. 55.
21. Louis Sigaud, *Belle Boyd: Confederate Spy* (Richmond, Virginia: Deitz Press, 1944) p. 14.
22. Ibid. p. 14.
23. Belle Boyd Hardinge, *Belle Boyd: The Recollections of a Famous Female Confederate Spy During the American Civil War* (UK: Leonaur LTD, 2019) p. 33.
24. Sigaud, *Belle Boyd: Confederate Spy*, p. 35.
25. Ibid. p. 49.
26. Ibid. p. 52.
27. Ibid. p. 74.
28. Ibid. p. 80.
29. Hardinge, *Belle Boyd: The Recollections of a Famous Female Confederate Spy During the American Civil War*, p. 80.
30. Sigaud, *Belle Boyd: Confederate Spy*, p. 154.
31. Ibid. p. 218.
32. S. Emma Edmonds, *Nurse and Spy in the Union Army: Memoirs* (Middletown, Delaware: ArtNow, 2020) p. 11.
33. Ibid. p. 11.
34. Ibid. p. 44.
35. Seymour Reit, *Behind Rebel Lines* (Boston: Clarion Books, 1988) p. 50.
36. Ibid. p. 126.
37. John Hendrix, *Nurse, Soldier, Spy* (New York: Abrams Books, 2011) p. 45.
38. Janet Huffmann, *The Clothesline Code* (Richmond, Virginia: Brandylane Publishers, 2021) p. 13.
39. Norman Schools, *Virginia Shade: An African American History of Falmouth, Virginia* (Bloomington, IN: iUniverse, 2012) p. 162.
40. Ibid. p. 162.
41. Ibid. p. 163.

42. Huffman, *The Clothesline Code*, p. 24
43. https://www.nationalww2museum.org/
44. James Buckley, Jr., *Who Were the Navajo Code Talkers?* (New York: Random House, 2021) p. 14.
45. Stuart Kallen, *Navajo Code Talkers* (Minneapolis, Minnesota: Lerner Publications, 2018) p. 11.
46. Buckley, Jr., *Who Were the Navajo Code Talkers?*, p. 30.
47. Ibid. p. 16.
48. Ibid. p. 42.
49. Kallen, *Navajo Code Talkers*, p. 21.
50. Buckley, Jr., *Who Were the Navajo Code Talkers?*, p. 61.
51. Kallen, *Navajo Code Talkers*, p. 23.
52. Ibid. p. 26.

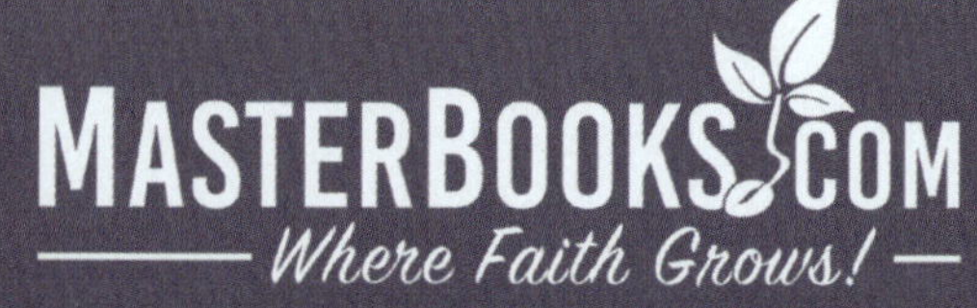